CIVICS FOR BARBADOS

CIVICS FOR BARBADOS

W. LeRoy Inniss

Cover photographs reproduced with the kind permission of the Government Information Service, Combermere School, Barbados Community College and UWI, Cave Hill.

Photographs on pages 95-99, reproduced with kind permission of the Government Information Service, Barbados.

Cover photographs reproduced with kind permission of the Government Information Service, Combermere School, Barbados Community College and UWI, Cave Hill.

Cover design by: Sanya Dockery
Book design, layout & typesetting by: Sanya Dockery

Published by: LMH Publishing Limited
7 Norman Road
LOJ Industrial Complex
Suite 10-11
Kingston C.S.O., Jamaica
Tel: 876-938-0005; 938-0712
Fax: 876-759-8752
Email: lmhbookpublishing
Website: www.lmhpublishing.com

Printed in the USA   ISBN: 978-976-8202-39-0

CONTENTS

FOREWORD

CIVICS FOR BARBADOS provides the reader with a wealth of information pertaining to the evolution and structure of political governance in Barbados. The collection of essays is written in a reader-friendly style employing an interactive technique. The author takes the reader on a journey from colony to independent nation state, in the process informing of the major challenges and achievements of a tiny country in a world dominated by megapowers.

The author succeeds in assisting the reader to appreciate why Barbados is regarded in international circles as one of the best-managed newly independent predominantly black states. He constantly reminds his audience that Barbados' achievements are not chance occurrences, but the result of visionary leadership, planning and sacrifice. Conscious of the value of Barbados' achievements and the fragility of democratic institutions, the author reminds us of the pivotal importance of public accountability, the role of an independent media, a professional civil service, and an independent judiciary to the continued growth and development of a Barbadian society in which divergent ideas will be permitted to flourish.

CIVICS FOR BARBADOS is a most valuable handbook for all Barbadians and other persons interested in becoming familiar with the fundamentals of Barbados' system of political governance and its major institutions. Barbadian society, and particularly the youth, will be well served by this publication. It is important that a people know the road they have travelled in order to arrive at the current national juncture. Ignorance of the road map can result in a loss of direction with severe national adverse consequences.

CIVICS FOR BARBADOS is an important contribution to the national compass. We are all indebted to Justice LeRoy Inniss for his contribution.

Professor Frank Alleyne

PREFACE

It is over 25 years since the first edition of this text was published. Since then, thousands of children and adults have used it as a source of material to familiarize them with the workings of the democratic system of government with special reference to our own society.

The text has been produced to provide readers in simple language with information designed to focus attention on the strengths and weaknesses of the system.

I wish to thank Ms. Natasha Griffith, attorney-at-law for her invaluable assistance in the production of this edition. In addition to ensuring that the material has been brought up to date, she has been responsible for the chapter on 'Our National Heroes'. The author remains, however, responsible for any defects in the work.

W. LeRoy Inniss
January 2007

INTRODUCTION
THE COUNTRY AND ITS PEOPLE

Barbados is a small pear-shaped island with an area of 166 square miles (approximately 430 square kilometres). It is 21 miles (approximately 34 kilometres) long by 14 miles (approximately 23 kilometres) wide at the widest part.

The island, which is the most easterly of the Caribbean archipelago, is located at latitude 13° North and longitude 59° West. The west coast has white sandy beaches and calm seas, while the cliff-lined Atlantic eastern coast is more turbulent. The island is generally flat, with parts of its interior and eastern coast known as the Scotland District being very hilly in nature. The land in the Scotland District rises to 335.5 metres or 1,100 feet high at Mount Hillaby, which is the highest point on the island.

Much of the island is comprised of coral and limestone, which add to its majestic scenery. Barbados is made of largely thick layers of limestone, with pockets of sand and clay. The whole island is virtually surrounded by coral reef and boast beautiful beaches, and an excellent network of roads and one of the best water systems in the world.

The entire country was once under sugar cultivation, as sugar was one of this country's biggest foreign exchange earners. The heyday of King Sugar has long passed and the tourist industry is now the largest foreign exchange earner. Barbados' financial services, manufacturing, oil and gas, agriculture, and non-trade sectors also contribute to this island's economic growth.

With a population of approximately 270,000, Barbados is one of the most densely populated countries in the world. Over 90 per cent of the inhabitants are of African descent. The ancestors of this group originated mainly from West Africa as slaves to work on the sugar plantations. The majority of the other inhabitants are Caucasian or people of mixed races. The members of the Caucasian population came from all walks of life. There were merchants and planters attracted by the riches, which they hoped to obtain from the cultivation of small plots, which they were given free of cost. There were also indentured servants who signed an agreement to work on a plantation for a fixed period of five or seven years in exchange for their passage to Barbados, food, clothes and shelter. In addition, political prisoners, nonconformists seeking religious freedom, and common convicts also formed part of the early population. During the 17th century, some Jews came to the island from Brazil and they were engaged to a large extent in lending money to the mercantile community. A small number of East Indians, Lebanese and Syrians arrived in Barbados during the early part of the 20th century. The vast majority of them are now involved in the dry goods business.

There is archaeological evidence that before Europeans came to Barbados, the island was the home of the peaceful Arawak Indians, who were probably driven out by the fiercer Caribs. After the departure of the Arawaks, the Caribs inhabited the island. Recent findings have revealed that another Indian tribe, the Ciboneys, also inhabited the island. In the Barbados Museum, there can be found pieces of Arawak pottery and implements. Artifacts of the Caribs were also discovered on the island.

It is believed that the first Europeans to visit Barbados were the Spaniards at the end of the 15th century. Neither they nor the Portuguese who followed in the 16th century settled, however. It was held for many years that, in 1625, English settlers arrived at Holetown on the *Olive Blossom* and claimed the island on behalf of England.

The generally accepted year of the first settlement in Barbados is now 1627. After that, Barbados remained in continuous British possession until it achieved political independence in 1966.

Originally, the early settlers cultivated tobacco and cotton, but during the 1640s when these crops received stiff competition from those of the North American colonies, they gave way to the cultivation of sugar cane, a change which brought with it the widespread importation of negro slaves from Africa. Life for the slaves was not easy on the plantation, and members of the Anti-Slavery Movement in England condemned the existence of slavery. This campaign was led by persons such as William Wilberforce and Thomas Buxton. In Barbados itself, an unsuccessful revolt was organized, in 1816, led by a free mulatto man, Washington Franklin, and the slave, Bussa. At last, in 1834, after almost two centuries of slavery, the slaves were emancipated.

During the 1870s, the planters experienced economic problems and this in turn led to hardship for the working classes. The British thought that if the governments of the West Indies were centralized they could be of greater assistance to the poor; thus they proposed creating a confederation between Barbados and the Windward Islands. One benefit of the proposed confederation, it was argued, would be the freedom to move from island to island. Barbadians would, therefore, be permitted to work Crown lands on some of the other islands. This suggestion was welcomed by the ex-slaves, but the proud Barbadian middle class led by Conrad Reeves (who later became the first coloured chief justice in the British Empire) rejected the proposal. The chief reason for the objection was that the proposal would cause Barbados to lose its Parliament of which it was proud. The resulting tensions eventually led to civil disturbances known as the Confederation Riots in 1876.

Monument at Holetown commemorating the landing of the first English settlers on the island.
(Photograph taken by Andrew Inniss)

Other disturbances came in the 1930s as a result of the social and economic conditions that existed at the time. Order was restored only after the loss of over a dozen lives. An important result of the disturbances was the formation for the first time of a political party and trade union on the island. This development was to transform the social and economic life of the country.

In 1958, Barbados joined with other islands of the West Indies in a British West Indies Federation, but this political union failed in 1962 when Jamaica seceded from the Federation. In 1966, the country gained its political independence from Britain and took its place as an independent member of the British Commonwealth. Since achieving independence, Barbados has joined the Organization of American States, the United Nations and other international organizations through which it is making its voice heard among the other independent nations of the world.

CHAPTER 1

THE DEVELOPMENT OF OUR SYSTEM OF GOVERNMENT

It is the right of the citizens of every country to decide for themselves the form of government which they wish to adopt. In Barbados, there is a democratic form of government based on the British system – this is known as the Westminster form of government. Today, every citizen of Barbados who is 18 years or older has the right to vote at general elections, which are due every five years. This right to vote was not constitutionally held by all the citizens and was only won after being fought for over several years.

In 1639, the first representative body was formed where representatives from among the freeholders sat as a legislative body with the Governor and a council appointed by him. Later in 1645, the island was divided into eleven parishes and two representatives were elected from each parish.

This early experience of parliamentary government has been responsible over the years for the proud boast that outside of Great Britain, Barbados possesses the second oldest legislature in the Commonwealth. However, that was not synonymous with a democratic system of government, for the vast majority of the population was excluded from participation in public affairs through the exercise of the franchise. In 1925, for example, of a total population of 156,311, only 3,496 were registered voters.

The right to vote was based on the ownership of the land. Thus until the introduction of universal adult suffrage, the socio-economic, as well as the political system, was completely dominated by the planter-merchant classes.

As late as 1936, a bill to reduce the income qualification for the franchise from £50 per annum to £30 per annum was rejected by the Legislative Council – a nominated body which was the forerunner of the Senate.

Skin colour also played an important part in deciding who could exercise the franchise. It was not before 1831 that free coloured men were allowed to vote and it took another nine years before legislation was passed to allow coloured men to sit in the House of Assembly. In 1843 when Samuel Jackman Prescod was elected to that body, he became the first coloured man to sit in the House of Assembly.

The worldwide economic depression of the 1930s aggravated the already deplorable condition of the masses. Their general dissatisfaction led to social unrest, which eventually brought to the fore champions of the working people's cause. One of their demands was the right for a greater number of the inhabitants of the country to exercise the franchise. This demand for widening the electoral roll was to have tremendous influence on the socio-economic development of the country, for as long as the legislature continued to be dominated by planters and merchants, the bulk of legislation passed would be designed to protect the interest of the ruling classes.

In 1944, the franchise was lowered from £50 to £20, thus allowing more persons to exercise the right to elect their representatives. At the same time, a further step forward was made when the right to vote was granted to women. In spite of the lowering of the franchise, many persons still remained disfranchised. In the general election of 1946, only 20,073 voters were registered out of a total population of over 192,000. These constitutional changes were followed by an experiment which came to be known as the "Bushe Experiment", so named after the then Governor, Sir Gratten Bushe. In an attempt to give greater power to the elected members of the House of Assembly to determine the affairs of the country, the Governor invited the leader of the majority party in the House of Assembly to name the members of the House who should sit on the Executive Committee. Members of the Executive Committee were then made responsible for the general policy of various government departments. Full representative government was eventually established in Barbados when there was universal adult suffrage, that is, when every citizen of 21 years and over had the right to vote for the members of the House of Assembly.

Although elected members of Parliament sat on the Executive Committee, the real power still resided in the hands of the Governor and his officials. In order for the will of the people to prevail, it was necessary for the crucial decisions to be made by their elected representatives. Control of the decision-making process was eventually transferred to the elected members by the introduction of ministerial government in 1954, when Mr. Grantley Adams (later Sir Grantley Adams) became the first Premier of Barbados. The transfer of power, from officials who were appointed to ministers who were elected by the people, was the foundation for social and economic change in the country.

In 1958, the Cabinet system of government was instituted. There was a further constitutional advance in 1961 when full internal self-government was achieved. With this advance, the Cabinet became responsible for all important matters affecting the country other than security and external affairs, which continued to be dealt with by the British Government.

The voting age was reduced from 21 to 18 years in 1963, and on November 30, 1966, Barbados became an independent nation. The first Prime Minister of independent Barbados was Mr. Errol Walton Barrow.

CHART A

POPULATION OF BARBADOS FOR THE YEARS
(1925-2005)

Year	Population
1925	156,311
1930	159,035
1935	168,971
1940	179,512
1945	191,291
1950	
1960	
1970	239,489
1980	249,424
1985	257.045
1990	261,525
1995	264,386
2000	269,321
2005	273,448

Source: Barbados Government Statistical Service Department (2006)

Source: West Indies Census 1946

CHART B

ELECTORAL ROLLS IN BARBADOS FOR THE YEARS

(1925-2003)

Year	Electorate
1925	3,496
1930	5,153
1935	5,564
1940	6,931
1945	20,073
1980	167,029
1990	185,873
1999	204,307
2003	220,093

Source: 1925 –1945 Barbados Blue Book

1980 – 2003 Register of Electors

CHAPTER 2

THE CITIZEN AND THE STATE

"The bond of Union is closer between those who belong to the same nation and closer still between those who are Citizens of the same state."

Cicero (106-43 B. C.)

Eligibility for Citizenship

With only a few exceptions, all persons are citizens of a state. Some persons are citizens of more than one state. The Constitution and the Barbadian Citizenship Act lay down the rules governing the acquisition and deprivation of Barbadian citizenship. It may be acquired by birth, descent from a Barbadian father (or in the case of children born out of wedlock to a Barbadian mother), by registration or by naturalization.

(a) By Birth   Section 4 of the Constitution states:
Every person born in Barbados after 29 November, 1966 shall become a citizen of Barbados at the date of the birth.

The section excludes persons whose parents possess diplomatic immunity if neither is a citizen of Barbados. It also excludes persons whose fathers are enemy aliens if the birth occurs in a place under enemy occupation.

(b) By Descent: According to Section 5 of the Constitution, the children born outside of Barbados of a man who is a citizen of Barbados become citizens at birth.

(c) By Registration: Section 6 makes provision for the wife of a Barbadian to be registered as a Barbadian citizen. There is no corresponding right for the husband of a Barbadian woman to be registered as a citizen by virtue of being married to a Barbadian. Many persons consider this as discrimination against women and argue that the Constitution should be amended to provide for equal rights for Barbadian women.

Other Commonwealth citizens who fulfil certain requirements may also apply for registration, and at the discretion of the minister, be registered as citizens.

(d) By Naturalization Non-Commonwealth citizens may apply to the Minister for naturalization provided they fulfil certain specific conditions. The minister has the discretion to grant or refuse naturalization.

The right to citizenship involves loyalty to the country of which one intends to be a citizen. Before a person, who is not a citizen by birth or descent, can become a citizen by naturalization, he or she has to take an oath of allegiance to the Sovereign.

Since citizenship entails loyalty, some countries hold that a person cannot owe allegiance to more than one country at the same time;

consequently they do not allow their citizens to hold citizenship of another country as well as theirs. Citizens of the United States of America for example, cannot apply for and hold citizenship of another country while retaining citizenship of their own country. Barbados permits dual citizenship; a Barbadian, therefore, does not have to renounce his citizenship to become a citizen of another country.

A Barbadian adult citizen may renounce his citizenship voluntarily, however, if he is at the same time, a citizen or national of another country or intends to become one. In some countries such as the former Soviet Union, for example, a citizen may be deprived of his citizenship, but in Barbados there is no way in which a person who is a citizen by birth or descent can lose his citizenship, except by renunciation. A citizen by registration or naturalization may be deprived of his citizenship at the discretion of the Minister.

The Good Citizen

We should be proud of the fact that we are citizens of a free democratic country such as Barbados and we should aim at making our community the best possible. We should all try to be good citizens. People differ in their opinion as to what characterizes a good citizen, but there are certain qualities which most people will accept as indicators of good citizenship.

As members of a community, we all have a part to play in the task of nation building. Every effort must be made in our democratic community to train citizens from their early days in the responsibilities of good citizenship. The first training ground is our home; this is where we experience our first feelings of belonging, and learn to share with others. It is in the home, too, that we are first introduced to justice and from where we learn patterns of social behaviour.

Later in the school, we continue to build on the foundation which was laid at home. The school probably has the greatest influence after the home in moulding the citizen. Not only are we taught the formal subjects at school, but we learn to live with others who are different from us. We come into contact with those who are more intelligent than we are, as well as some who are less intelligent. By participating in games, we develop the habit of teamwork and learn how to accept defeat with good grace. Today, the school also provides students with examples of democracy and self-government by allowing them to choose their class monitors, prefects and other school officers. School councils composed of members of the senior forms influence the decisions that are made with regard to the rules and regulations of the school. All those experiences help us to become good and responsible citizens and lay the groundwork for the society in which we live.

The Rights of a Citizen

One of the principal rights of a Barbadian citizen is the right to participate in the Government of his country, either by offering himself as a candidate for election to Parliament or by voting for others to represent him. In addition to these rights, the citizen is protected by the ordinary laws of the land and cannot be lawfully arrested or detained unless he is suspected of having committed some wrong. If he has been unlawfully arrested or detained he may seek redress before the court. The citizen also has the right to join any trade union or political organization of his choice and enjoys freedom of speech and freedom of worship. He may publish anything provided in doing so he is not in breach of any existing law. The Constitution guarantees his right to own property and he has the right to protect himself, his family and his property.

Citizenship also carries with it the privilege of holding a passport of Barbados and being entitled to the assistance of Barbadian consulates and embassies abroad. A citizen cannot be denied the right to return to the country at any time and, unlike the case in some other countries, he may move freely from one part of the country to another without having to seek permission from the authorities to do so.

Barbados, like most other countries, ensures that its citizens are accorded priority in the field of employment. Non-citizens must apply for work permits, which are normally granted only if there is no suitably qualified Barbadian available to fill the particular position.

We should note that a non-citizen or alien who is living in Barbados enjoys many of the privileges of the citizen, such as freedom from arbitrary arrest, freedom of worship and freedom of speech. He does not possess all the rights of a citizen, however, such as the right to hold a Barbadian passport. He may also be expelled from the country if it becomes necessary.

In early Athens, the members of the community took pride in their society and all participated in the social events as well as the Government of their communities. Today, it is not practicable for everyone to participate in the actual decision-making process, so we elect persons to represent us in the Government. The good citizen, however, still takes an interest in his society and participates in its activities as much as he can. Let us see some of the things that may be expected of a good citizen.

We have already learnt that an important privilege of the adult citizen is to select his representatives. The good citizen, therefore, is expected to participate in elections and vote for his representatives. The vote should be exercised in favour of a candidate, not because of any bribes which may be offered, for the right to vote is one which is too precious to be bought. Rather, the vote should be exercised in favour of the candidate who the citizen thinks will best serve the interest of the people. It is, therefore, necessary that the voter, before exercising his right, discuss the various issues involved and keep himself informed of what is happening in the country. Jose Martí, the Cuban poet, wrote: "When good men are indifferent, bad men triumph." These words should serve to remind us of the importance of casting our votes wisely. We should ensure that unsuitable persons are not elected to Parliament simply because we are too indifferent to elect suitable persons.

A good citizen will pay his share of the cost of managing his country. He will, therefore, pay his taxes and not try to defraud the Revenue Department, neither will he try to live off his fellow citizens, but will do all in his power to assist in building his community.

He develops traits of industry and would never remain unemployed when there is the opportunity to work, for he would not want to be a charge on the society. Often we see persons stealing or destroying property which they claim is "government property". We must remember that all such property does not belong to a political party or to the elected members of the public. When we abuse public property, we are really hurting ourselves, for the money it takes to replace it could have been better spent in providing further benefits for the community. The good citizen will take pride in protecting public property and in encouraging others to do so.

Many people see participation in organizations such as the Parent Teachers' Association and other voluntary organizations as signs of good citizenship. The good citizen would keep foremost in his mind the words of the late American President, John Fitzgerald Kennedy: "Ask not what your country can do for you, but what you can do for your country."

The good citizen will show consideration for his neighbours and will be tolerant to those whose religious or political beliefs or way of life differs from his own. He will support the right of every one to have freedom of speech, provided that what is said is not defamatory of other members of the community. The good citizen will always strive to see that the conditions which prevail in his society will ensure a better life for all.

An important responsibility of the good citizen is to obey the laws of the land, and to assist the authorities in seeing that justice is done. He will not do wrong to his neighbour, neither will he refrain from speaking out against the wrongdoings of others.

It is the citizen's duty to assist the police in maintaining law and order, and he is even given the opportunity by the state to assist in the administration of justice. One important means by which this opportunity is permitted is in the working of the jury system. For many years, the British system of justice which we have adopted held that an accused man should be judged as we know it today. The good citizen when called upon to perform jury service will not regard it as an imposition, but rather as a privilege which should be readily accepted.

Many of the duties of the citizen are voluntary and cannot be enforced in the courts. Good citizenship is, therefore, often a matter of conscience and is based on a sense of responsibility.

EXERCISES

1.   Suggest some ways in which a citizen can serve his community.

2.   Explain the privileges and duties of a citizen.

3.   What qualities would you look for in selecting prefects at your school?

4.   "The lack of provision for the husbands of Barbadian women to be automatically registered as Barbadian citizens is discriminatory against Barbadian women. The Constitution should be amended to include such a right." Discuss.

CHAPTER 3

HOW WE ARE GOVERNED

"Government of the people by the people for the people shall not perish from the earth.

Abraham Lincoln (1809-1865)

The Constitution

When we become members of a club or society, we notice that there are certain rules and regulations stating how the organization is to be governed. These rules and regulations form the constitution of the organization. Some countries such as Barbados, the United States of America, Guyana and Jamaica have their constitutions in written form, while other countries do not. Britain is a notable example of a country which has no written constitution. Nowadays, it is customary for countries which achieve their independence to have written constitutions.

The constitution of a country is very important, and in order to ensure that it is not changed at the whim and fancy of any government which is in power at a particular time, the constitution itself normally contains special procedures for its amendment. Some provide for the affirmative resolution of a two-thirds majority of Parliament to change the constitution or some important parts of it, while others demand a referendum. Whatever method is used, it is not usual for a constitution to be changed by a simple majority vote of Parliament.

Barbados became independent on November 30, 1966. From that date, the Constitution of Barbados became the supreme law of the land; all other laws get their authority from it and are subject to it. If

Parliament attempts to pass a law which is not in keeping with the Constitution, such a law would be declared "unconstitutional" by the law courts. For example, the Constitution provides that it is necessary to have the support of a two-thirds majority in Parliament to amend certain of its sections. If Parliament should attempt to change any of these clauses of the Constitution in any manner other than that laid down by the Constitution, Parliament's action would be illegal and the enactment would be declared by the court to be null and void. In 1993, for example, the courts decided that sections of the Landlord and Tenant (Registration of Tenancies) Act were unconstitutional.

This power of the court to overrule certain enactments of Parliament is one difference between the British Parliament, which is supreme and can pass any law it desires, and the Barbados Parliament. In Barbados, as in the case of other Commonwealth countries with written constitutions, Parliament is subject to the Constitution.

Besides declaring who are or who can become citizens of Barbados, the Constitution also provides for the protection of fundamental rights and freedoms of the individual. Some of the rights and freedoms guaranteed are:

(a)   the right to life, liberty and the security of the person;
(b)   protection for the privacy of the home and other property;
(c)   protection of the law;
(d)   freedom of conscience, of expression, of assembly and association.

The Constitution also protects all citizens from discrimination on grounds of race, origin, or political opinion. In addition, it provides for the functioning of the Governor-General, the Cabinet, and the Parliament of the country.

There are certain important clauses of the Constitution which may only be amended by the vote of two-thirds majority of the members of both Houses of Parliament. These clauses are known as entrenched clauses and are designed for the protection of the citizen. We have

PREAMBLE

BARBADOS CONSTITUTION

Whereas the love of free institutions and of independence has always strongly marked the inhabitants of Barbados:

And whereas the Governor and the said inhabitants settled a Parliament in the year 1639:

And whereas as early as February 16, 1651 these inhabitants, in their determination to safeguard the freedom, safety and well-being of the island declared, through their Governor, Lord of the Council and members of the Assembly, their independence of the Commonwealth of England:

And whereas the rights and privileges of the said inhabitants were confirmed by articles of agreement commonly known as the Charter of Barbados, had been made and concluded on January 11, 1652 by and between the Commissions of Right Honourable the Lord Willoughby of Parham, Governor of the one part, and the Commissioners on the behalf of the Commonwealth of England, of the said island of Barbados.

And whereas with the broadening down of freedom of the people of Barbados have ever since then not only successfully resisted any attempt to impugn or diminish those rights and privileges so confirmed, but have consistently enlarged and extended them:

Now, therefore, the people of Barbados

(a)   proclaim that they are a sovereign nation founded upon principles that acknowledge the supremacy of God, the dignity of the human person, their unshakable faith in fundamental human rights and freedom, the position of the family in a society of free men and institutions;

(b)   affirm their belief that men and institutions remain free ...

Preamble to the Barbados Constitution

already seen that certain parts of the Constitution can only be altered on an affirmative vote of at least two-thirds of all the members of Parliament; this is one of the entrenched clauses. Some other entrenched clauses are those guaranteeing the fundamental rights and freedoms of the individual. It is important to have these civil rights entrenched in the Constitution, so that it would be very difficult for a particular political party to have them removed and thus jeopardize our democratic way of life. Any attempt by government to violate the citizen's rights can be brought before the ordinary courts for justice to be done. Unfortunately, some poor persons are not able to vindicate their rights because of the expense involved sometimes in seeking justice before the courts. It is necessary for government to provide legal aid to all persons who have need to seek the assistance of the court, but do not have the means with which to do so. There is also the office of the ombudsman. His duty is to receive and deal with complaints made by the citizen against government ministers and other officials of government departments.

The Ombudsman

In Barbados, the Ombudsman Act, Chapter 8A of the laws of Barbados provides for the establishment of the post of ombudsman of Barbados. The creation of this post is of great significance as from time to time persons have been known to suffer some injustice at the hands of government officers. The office of ombudsman was created to eradicate these injustices as far as possible. The ombudsman has power to investigate to ascertain whether injustice has been caused by improper, unreasonable and inadequate administrative conduct on the part of a government ministry or department or other authority subject to the Ombudsman Act. It should be noted that the ombudsman cannot investigate a case where the complainant would have had as remedy a right of appeal, in a court of law or tribunal, unless he is satisfied that for some special reason the complainant could not be expected to have recourse to such a remedy or right of appeal.

The ombudsman deals with all complaints against all those persons vested with executive power. This office can strengthen the existing human rights institutions and make government agencies more transparent and accountable.

Public Officers Entrenched in the Constitution

It has been thought necessary, for reasons which we will learn of later, that the appointment and functioning of certain public officers should be specifically provided for in the Constitution; consequently, the establishment of the office of Governor-General and his functions, the protection of tenure and functioning of judges, the Director of Public Prosecutions and the Auditor-General, and the establishment and composition of the Service Commissions are entrenched in the Constitution. It is the Constitution, too, which makes it mandatory for all government revenue to be paid into a consolidated fund. It also provides for annual estimates and stipulates the legal manner in which public money may be expended.

Constitutional Amendments

Barbados' Constitution is now 40 years old. Some amendments have been made to the original constitution, the most notable being in 1974. However, its basic features remain unchanged. In October 1994, the Prime Minister, the Right Honourable Owen Arthur, announced that a commission to review the Constitution would be established, in an effort to improve the governance of Barbados and to strengthen our democratic institutions.

On October 29, 1996, in keeping with that commitment, the Constitutional Review Commission, under the chairmanship of Sir Henry Forded Q.C; M.P; was appointed to review the Constitution.

This commission was made up of outstanding Barbadians reflecting all shades of opinion, including members of the clergy, past members of the judiciary, educators and lay persons. It was mandated amongst other things to determine the necessity for retaining the monarchical system of government and to make recommendations in respect of the executive form of government.

In 1998, the commission published a report detailing its various recommendations. One such recommendation was a proposal for Barbados to become a republican state and that a referendum be held to determine the public opinion on the issue. A referendum is a constitutional device sometimes used when the government proposes to make significant change to the system of Government or to the constitution that wider public opinion is necessary. The referendum will be conducted in the same manner as a general election in Barbados.

Following the publication of the commission's report, there was much public debate on the question of a referendum on the question of republican status for this country. In 2005, the Referendum Act 2005-23 was passed in Parliament, outlining the procedure for the proposed referendum on republican status.

Should the proposed question of the referendum of republican status for this country be answered by the electorate in the affirmative, and the Government accepts the decisions, there are certain changes which will be made to our system of government. These changes include:

(a) The declaration of Barbados as a parliamentary republic;

(b) The removal of the British monarch, as our head of state,

(c) The removal of the Governor-General as the Queen's representative in Barbados,

(d) The appointment of a president, who is a citizen of Barbados as our head of state and

(e) This nation's citizens will no longer have to swear oaths of allegiance to the British monarch. For example, at present, the Prime Minister and other members of the Cabinet swear allegiance to the Queen. Similarly, jurors will cease to swear that they will deliver a true verdict in the matter between "our sovereign Lady the Queen and the Accused".

How We Choose Our Representatives

We have learnt that Barbados has a democratic form of government. Democracy was described by Abraham Lincoln in his famous address at Gettysburg as a form of government of the people, by the people, for the people.

Besides being a form of government which provides for the will of the majority to prevail, democracy implies many important traditions. These include freedom of the press, free and open discussions on matters of public interest, and freedom to choose the political party or candidate of one's choice. Citizens in a democracy, therefore, are involved in the Government of their country.

Since, as we have said earlier, it is not possible in modern society for the whole community to meet and decide matters of importance, we choose representatives who make important decisions on our behalf. Various people have different ideas as to how these representatives should be chosen; some believe that only the most educated or wealthy should represent the community, while others believe that representatives should be chosen only by those who make worthwhile contributions to the community or who own property. For many years in some countries such as South Africa, the race of the inhabitant has been relevant in deciding what part he should play in the Government of the country. We have chosen to select our representatives by free elections which are constitutionally held at intervals of not more than five years. In that way, we have the opportunity to review the work of representatives, change those with whose work we are not satisfied, and elect persons who offer a programme of which we approve.

One must not be misled, however, into believing that every country which holds a form of elections or which calls itself 'democratic' is a true democracy. Some of the most undemocratic countries of the world have the word 'Democratic' as part of their name. The true test of democracy is the active participation of the citizens in the decision-making process at national levels.

Some critics of this form of government claim that the only time the ordinary citizens participate in government is a few seconds, every five years, when they cast their votes. This ought not to be so, for the alert citizen should remain informed and vigilant, use the press and other means to point out when the elected members are not keeping their promises or acting in contravention of the mandate given by the electorate.

In addition, the fact that the electorate has the right in the future to change the Government, acts as some check on the conduct of parliamentarians. Some persons claim that five years is too long to wait to show one's disapproval of the actions of an inefficient representative. One way of overcoming this is by providing that a representative can be recalled if a certain number of his constituents ask for it. This may be attractive in theory, but one difficulty is that in a system where there is the right of recall, opposition members may use the system as a means of preventing a government from functioning efficiently, by requesting frequent recall of members.

One of the greatest dangers of democracy is a government which has all the appearances of democracy, but in which the politicians do not observe the true practices and spirit of this system. Some ways of undermining democracy are:

(a)   Having regular elections, but rigging or falsifying the polls, or preventing opposition candidates from campaigning freely.

(b)   Controlling the media and allowing only propaganda favourable to the Government to be disseminated.

(c)   Falsifying electoral lists.

(d)   Proclaiming freedom of speech while those who speak against the Government are discriminated against in the field of work, education, housing and the distribution of other necessities.

Before we can vote it is first necessary to be registered. At present, every citizen who is 18 years old or over, and is not a prisoner, or of unsound mind, or has not been disqualified by a competent court from voting, is entitled to be registered and to vote at all elections for Parliament. This right to vote is called having the franchise. Since virtually every adult has the right to vote, the system is known as "universal adult suffrage".

The management of the entire electoral system is in the hands of the Electoral and Boundaries Commission. This is a body comprising five persons: the Chairman and two members who are appointed by the Governor-General on the advice of the Prime Minister, and two other members who are appointed by the Governor-General on the advice of the Leader of the Opposition. The commission has the responsibility for the conduct of elections. It is also responsible for submitting for the approval of Parliament, the number of constituencies into which the island is to be divided and the boundaries of each constituency.

The chief electoral officer is responsible for the administration of the Electoral Office. A register of all persons eligible to vote is kept in this office. It is the duty of the citizen to see that his name appears on the register. Persons may register at any time throughout the year, but when a general election is near at hand, sometimes persons called enumerators go from house to house to register those persons who are not yet registered. These lists are displayed for the benefit of the public and anyone whose name does not appear can make sure that he is registered. After registration, the citizen is photographed and issued with an identification card. The electoral register is revised regularly to ensure that persons who reached the voting age are included, while those who have left the country are disqualified from voting, and those who have died are excluded. The revision also notes the necessary changes when persons move from one district to another.

Publication of the list of electors is an important safeguard and is vital to the maintenance of confidence in the electoral system. Every effort should be made to allow proper scrutiny by political parties and individuals, to ensure that the electoral list is not padded with names of persons who are non-existent, below the voting age or are otherwise disqualified.

For the purposes of elections, the country is at present divided into 30 areas known as constituencies. Parliament has the power to increase or reduce the number of constituencies. Each constituency is represented by one member in Parliament. When it is time for an election to be held, a day known as Nomination Day is fixed. On that day, two registered voters of each constituency nominate a person who will contest the election on polling day. The nomination is further supported by two other registered voters of the constituency. Any citizen who is eligible to vote may be nominated. While it is possible for candidates to enter the electoral race as independents, very seldom nowadays is an Independent elected, for anyone who is not sure of a party to support his programmes cannot guarantee that he would be able to carry out the promises made to the voters, if he is elected. Persons are usually sponsored, therefore, by a political party.

Before a person is nominated, he has to deposit BDS $250.00 into the Government Treasury. If he eventually receives at least one-eighth of the votes cast in the constituency he recovers it, otherwise his deposit is forfeited. The reason for this deposit is to discourage frivolous nominations.

Political Parties and Elections

We have already seen that the Constitution guarantees every citizen the right to join a political party of his choice. The party system is a healthy feature in a democracy since it can provide the electorate with a real choice of alternative candidates. The Constitution gives no

NOMINATION PAPER

Form 3

(Rule 5(1))

ELECTION OF MEMBER to serve in the House of Assembly for the Constituency of...

We, the undersigned, being electors for the said Constituency, do hereby nominate the under-mentioned person as a candidate at the said election.

Candidate's Surname	Other names in full	Place of Residence	Description

Proposer (Signature) ....

Seconder (Signature) ....

Election Number
(See Note 4)
....

We, the undersigned, being electors for the said Constituency, do hereby assent to the foregoing nomination.

1. (Signature) ....

2. (Signature) ....

NOTE

1.	The attention of candidates and electors is drawn to the rules for filling up nomination papers and other provisions relating to nomination contained in the election rules in the Second Schedule to the Representation of the People Act, Chapter 12 of the Laws of Barbados.

2.	Where a candidate is commonly known by some title he may be described by his title as if it were his surname.

3.	An elector may not subscribe more than one nomination paper for the same election.

4.	A person's electoral number is his number in the Register used at the Election (including the distinctive letter or letters (if any) of the polling district in which he is registered) except that before publication of the Registers his number, (if any), in the annual or revised lists shall be used instead.

A sample of a nomination paper.

direct recognition to the existence of political parties, but they are indirectly recognized by the provisions governing the choice of Prime Minister and by the institution of the office of the Leader of the Opposition. Since the principal aim of the party is to ensure the election of Members of Parliament, to this end it organizes meetings, distributes propaganda and uses the news media to publicize its views and to convince the public to vote for its members. The programme, which each political party promises the electorate to implement, if it is selected to form the Government, is set out in a document known as a manifesto. A common feature of Barbados' political life is the public meeting at which the leaders and the candidates of the various parties address gatherings of persons, seeking their support at the elections.

At the conclusion of a general election the party which wins the majority of seats forms the Government, and the leader of that party usually becomes the Prime Minister. He, along with some of the principal members of the party, forms the Cabinet.

The Election

On election day there are various polling stations located within each constituency for the convenience of the electors. Each polling station is headed by an official known as the presiding officer, who is assisted by a number of clerks. Also present in the polling station are representatives of each candidate who is contesting the election in the

BALLOT PAPER FRONT FORM OF BALLOT PAPER		
1	BROWN JOHN THOMAS BROWN	
2	JONES PHILLIP WILLIAM JONES	
3	SMITH MARY JANE SMITH	

particular constituency. It is the duty of these representatives to see that nothing is done prejudicial to the interest of their candidates. The voter goes to the polling station to which he is assigned to cast his vote. After the presiding officer is satisfied as to his identity, he gives him a ballot paper on which he casts his vote. This is done in secret by marking an X beside the name of the candidate he wants to see elected. After the voter has done this, he folds his ballot paper and places it into the ballot box provided for that purpose. If he makes more than one mark or allows his X to touch the lines, the vote is spoilt and will be rejected at counting time.

In some countries, especially those which have a high rate of illiteracy, party symbols such as a bell, a star, or a torch are placed beside the name of the candidate. This is done to help the voter to recognize the candidate who is representing the party which he intends to support, since each party usually has the same symbol for all its candidates. In Barbados, no symbols appear on the ballot paper; only the names of the candidates are used. Persons who are blind or otherwise incapacitated may seek the assistance of the presiding officer or take a relative to the polls to assist him or her in casting his or her vote. Illiterate persons may also request the presiding officer to make their mark next to the name of the person for whom they wish to vote. This is a very serious responsibility, and for that reason, only persons of the highest integrity should be selected as presiding officers.

After the poll has been closed, the votes are counted and the candidate who receives the highest number of votes is declared winner by the official in charge of the election in the particular constituency. This officer is known as the returning officer. If an unsuccessful candidate is not satisfied with the result, he may ask for a recount. Normally, this is only done if the victory is by a narrow margin.

In a true democracy, every effort is made to ensure that the person selected to represent the people is really the one whom the majority of voters have freely chosen; therefore, measures are taken to prevent an elector from casting more than one vote or doing any other illegal act. Every effort is also made to ensure that the voter is not unduly influenced when making his choice of a candidate. To prevent this, certain rules must be observed on election day:

1. No one is allowed to campaign on the day of election.

2. Party flags and other advertising material cannot be displayed.

3. No alcoholic drink may be sold during the time the votes are being cast.

4.   No persons are allowed to gather within 100 yards of a polling station.

After the election, if a candidate in the election can produce evidence to prove that his opponent was guilty of some illegal practice to secure his election, or if he is dissatisfied with the count, he may bring a petition in law to have the election declared null and void or to have himself declared winner of the seat.

Sometimes, we hear persons saying that they have no interest in politics and will not vote for any candidate. This is a wrong attitude for often bad people are elected who are not suitable because the good would not exercise their right to vote. In some countries, for example, Belgium and Australia, all persons eligible to vote are compelled by law to do so, failing which, they are fined. In Barbados voting is voluntary. Nevertheless, all eligible citizens should exercise their right to vote since in this way we may decide peaceably whom we wish to manage our affairs. In order that every voter is given the opportunity to cast his vote, the law provides for employers to grant time off to all employees on polling day. We must remember that rights, like freedom of worship and freedom of speech, which we take for granted, can only be guaranteed by the political system. If we are not vigilant, a system which removes these rights may be introduced at anytime. The saying of Abraham Lincoln that "the ballot is stronger than the bullet" vividly reminds us of the power of the vote.

If a Member of Parliament resigns before he has served his full term in Parliament or if a member dies or is disqualified from taking his seat for some reason, it then becomes necessary to hold an election to fill the vacancy. These elections which are held at any time other than that of a general election are known as by-elections. A by-election is conducted in the same manner as a general election.

The system of declaring the winner to be the candidate with the highest number of votes in each constituency is known as first-past-the-post system. Under this system, it is possible for a political party to form a government without having received a majority of the votes cast in the country, while another party can receive a high percentage of votes and still obtain no seat in Parliament. If, for example, one party wins all of its seats by very narrow margins, but is heavily defeated in the constituencies where it loses, the total result could show that the losing party had a higher percentage of the total votes cast in the country. Again, a party could win all the seats in the country by a small majority in each constituency, thus leaving the view of a large minority unrepresented in Parliament. In 1956, the Barbados Labour Party won 49% of the vote, but gained 63% of the seats in Parliament. In 1991, the Democratic Labour Party won 50% of the votes and 64% of the seats. In 1999, the Barbados Labour Party won 64.8% of the vote and gained 93% of the seats in Parliament. In 2003, the Barbados Labour Party won 56.3% of the votes and 77% of the seats.

Imagine there is an election in which there are four candidates. At the end of the election the votes cast for the various candidates are as follows:-

Candidate	No. Votes Secured
JONES	12,000
BROWNE	10,000
SMITH	9,000
WHITE	6,000

In the above case, while 12,000 persons voted for Jones, he was not the preferred candidate of 25,000 of the voters, yet, because he obtained the highest single number of votes he would be declared the winner of the election. It may be argued, that, in such a case, the will of the electorate has not really been reflected in the composition of Parliament.

In order to avoid such a situation, various other methods have been designed. One is by means of a second ballot. In this system, if a candidate does not receive more than 50% of the votes cast, a second ballot is held, where the only candidates are the two who received the highest number of votes in the first ballot.

This system, however, can also be criticized on the ground that the final two candidates were not chosen by a majority of the electorate, but rather by a procedure which eliminated some of the other candidates.

Some countries have sought to ensure that minorities are represented in Parliament by adopting a system of "proportional representation". Under this system, the seats in Parliament are divided in the same proportions as the votes cast.

It would not be possible, therefore, for a single party to form the Government without receiving a majority of the national votes; neither would minority parties be excluded from Parliament. There are some objections, however, to this system. It is very likely that since no one party would be able to form a government, a coalition would become necessary. This could lead to compromises, with parties not being able to carry out the programmes which were promised to the electorate. Parties might be tempted to make all types of promises which they cannot fulfil and when they fail to carry out their promises, blame the failure on the fact that they had to make sacrifices to satisfy their coalition partners.

There would most likely be a proliferation of parties since this system offers greater opportunity for minority parties to be elected to Parliament. Another disadvantage of proportional representation is that it encourages delay and extreme caution, since a coalition government is less likely to act as quickly and boldly as a government which has a strong parliamentary majority. Some countries adopt a system which combines proportional representation and first-past-the-post.

Whatever may be the weaknesses of the different forms of electing representatives, the most important thing is that, in our system of government, the entire adult population has the right to participate in the choice of the political directorate.

Below is a table showing the distribution of votes cast and the number and precentage of seats won by the various political parties in general elections 1981-2003.

Year	BLP		DLP		NDP	
	% votes received	% seats won	% votes received	% seats won	% votes received	% seats won
1981	52.2	63	47.1	37	-	-
1986	40.4	11	59.4	89	-	-
1991	42.5	36	50.3	64	-	-
1994	48.3	68	38.3	29	12.8	3
1999	64.8	93	35	7	-	-
2003	56.3	77	43.6	23	-	-

EXERCISES

1. (a)   Name the constituencies in Barbados and state which Member of Parliament represents each constituency.

    (b)   Can you think of any other rights which are not in the present Constitution, but which should have been included?

2. (a)   Why do you think voters are allowed to cast their votes in secret?

    (b)   If Barbados became a republic should the President be ceremonial or executive? Why?

    (c)   What are the advantages and disadvantages of the system in which one man has one vote?

    (d)   Do you think that there is a place in our present system for independent Members of Parliament?

3.   Debate: The system of first-past-the-post provides a strong government rather than a democratic government.

CHAPTER 4
THE GOVERNMENT

*Government is a trust and the Officers of Government are trustees and both
the trust and the trustees are created for the benefit of 'the people"*

Henry Clay (1777-1852)

The Governor-General

Just as clubs and societies hold general meetings and elect officers
and committees of management, certain persons are elected and given
the responsibility of managing the affairs of a country.

Barbados is a constitutional monarchy with a parliamentary system
of government. At the head of our Government is the Queen, who is
represented in Barbados by a Governor-General whom she appoints
on the advice of the Prime Minister. Neither the Queen nor the
Governor-General, however, is responsible for making the important
decisions in the country.

The Governor-General's functions, such as the conferring of honours
and the receiving of ambassadors, are mainly ceremonial. In addition,
he has certain functions which are prescribed by the Constitution. With
a few exceptions, these functions must be exercised on the advice of the
Prime Minister. A few are exercised on the advice of the Prime
Minister after consultation with the Leader of the Opposition. The
appointment of the chief justice, for example, is done in that manner.
In appointing two of the members of the Senate, as we will see later, the
Governor-General acts on the advice of the Leader of the Opposition.

Two functions which the Governor-General exercises in his own discretion are the appointment of a Prime Minister and the appointment of seven members of the Senate. Normally, there is no problem in choosing the Prime Minister since the leader of the party which has won a majority of seats in an election will be appointed to that position. If, however, there is a close election where no party has an outright majority, the Governor-General might have the opportunity to really exercise his discretion. The Governor of St. Vincent was called upon to make that kind of decision in 1972. Since the Governor-General is appointed and may be removed on the advice of the Prime Minister, it is unlikely that in appointing the seven members to the Senate in his own discretion, he would appoint persons all of whom are opposed to the Government in power.

At the beginning of each new session of Parliament, the Governor-General makes a speech outlining the plans the Government hopes to implement during the course of the session. This speech, which is known as the Throne Speech, is prepared by the members of the Cabinet with the assistance of senior civil servants.

There is provision in the Constitution for the Governor-General to appoint an advisory body known as the Privy Council. This body, which must not be confused with Her Majesty's Privy Council in London, is appointed after consultation with and not on the advice of the Prime Minister. In 1978, in Jamaica there was some controversy when it was learnt that the Governor-General, in exercise of a similar discretion, appointed members of his Privy Council contrary to the advice of the Prime Minister. Some sections of the community argued that although the matter was within the absolute discretion of the Governor-General, this discretion should not be exercised contrary to the will of the leader of the elected government. Others argued, on the other hand, that the Governor-General should be unfettered in the exercise of his discretion since this would assist, even though in a small way, in placing some check on the power of the Prime Minister.

Two of the most important functions of the Privy Council are to hear appeals from civil servants who have been disciplined, as well as to recommend to the Governor-General the remission of sentence of persons who have been convicted in the law courts. The Privy Council also considers petitions for the exercise of the prerogative of mercy from persons who have been sentenced to death by the court. If this prerogative is exercised, the death sentence is commuted to a term of imprisonment.

Ministers of Government

The real power of government, however, is in the hands of the Prime Minister and his Cabinet. Only the Prime Minister has the right to select or dismiss members of the Cabinet. Ministers may be chosen from either the House of Assembly or from the Senate.

The Cabinet consists of the Prime Minister and a number of ministers, each one responsible for the political management of the department which comes under his ministry; for example, Finance, Trade and Tourism and so on. The list of subjects for which the minister is responsible is known as his portfolio and he has to defend in Parliament the Government's policy in respect of the matters that form his portfolio. Sometimes a Minister of State or Minister 'without portfolio' is appointed. These ministers assist other ministers with the matters which fall within their portfolios.

Major matters are brought before Cabinet for discussion and approval. Cabinet discussions are important for often one particular matter involves several ministers; for example, if the decision is taken by the Minister of Education to build a new school, the Minister of Finance must approve the funds, while the Ministry of Communications and Works may be responsible for the actual construction and the ministry responsible for the civil service may have to make provisions for staffing it. If any legal matters arise in the arrangements, they have to be referred to the attorney-general.

It is Cabinet, therefore, which has the responsibility for deciding how the country should be governed. One of the principles of Cabinet Government is collective responsibility, that is, that the entire Cabinet is held responsible for the policy of the Government. Matters discussed by Cabinet are confidential and after a decision is taken on a matter, no Minister is in a position to say that he disagrees with a particular aspect of the policy. If a minister finds that he cannot accept the collective decision of the Cabinet, his duty is to resign. Sometimes, the Prime Minister takes particular duties from a minister and assigns different ones to him: he may bring in a new minister to relieve an existing minister of his duties; this is known as 'reshuffling' his Cabinet.

Besides members of the Cabinet, there are also junior ministers, sometimes called parliamentary secretaries. They, like the senior ministers, may be drawn from either House of Parliament. They assist some ministers in carrying out their functions, but they are not members of the Cabinet.

The position of Prime Minister is one of great importance and power. The holder of this office has several functions including the following:

1. (a)   The decision, in his own discretion, about when a general election is to be held at any time within the constitutional five-year life of Parliament;
    (b)   The recommendation to the Governor-General for the appointment and dismissal of members of the Cabinet at will;
    (c)   The appointment of 12 members of the Senate;
    (d)   The recommendation to the Governor-General for the appointment of certain office holders including the chief justice and other judges of the High Court.

2. The recommendation to the Governor-General for the appointment of permanent secretaries and heads of government departments;

3. The appointment of foreign service officers on his recommendation.

Besides the direct power conferred by the Constitution, the Prime Minister has the additional inevitable advantage of any person who has the right to appoint others to positions of relative wealth, prestige and power. The holder of the post of Prime Minister should recognize that besides giving him privilege and power, the office also presents a tremendous responsibility. He should not be tempted into using his power for his personal benefit and that of his friends, but rather, should exercise it for the good of the nation. Some argue, and with some merit, that a strong Prime Minister, who surrounds himself with underlings who are dependent on him for their position and personal financial success, may very well become a dictator while pretending to preside over a democratic form of government. The citizens must be careful, therefore, to ensure that only a person with the correct character, integrity and ability holds this office.

At election time, the elector must recognize that he is voting not only for his individual representative, but for a Prime Minister and his Cabinet. It is, therefore, absolutely necessary to examine the leaders of each party, as well as their list of candidates, to determine if they can be considered worthy of forming a government.

Whenever we refer to the Government as "they" and ask why don't "they" do this and why don't "they" do that?", we should remember that the members of the Government are only acting on our behalf. We take part indirectly in the Government of the country, when at election time, we elect those whose policy we approve of and change those leaders who fail to carry out their promises or who put forward programmes of which we do not approve. Since these leaders are elected to represent us, they are responsible to us for the management of the country. The ordinary citizen, therefore, should not regard democracy as a system of government in which inhabitants exercise the right to vote every five years and have nothing else to do until another election is called. His responsibilities do not end with the election of his Member of Parliament.

The citizen in a democratic society needs to be vigilant to ensure that his will is being recognized. He has the right to ask his representative why things are not done or why they are done in a particular manner.

Parliament

Some countries have a Parliament consisting of one body of persons; this is known as unicameral legislature. Others have two different bodies. When Parliament consists of two chambers, it is known as bicameral legislature, for example, Guyana has a unicameral legislature while Trinidad and Tobago has a bicameral legislature.

In Barbados, Parliament consists of two bodies known as the House of Assembly, which is elected and a nominated Upper Chamber known as the Senate.

We have already learnt that as early as 1645 the country was divided into 11 parishes and each parish elected two representatives to Parliament. In 1843, the City of Bridgetown was granted the right to elect its own representatives. From that time the House of Assembly consisted of 24 elected members; two from each of the 11 parishes and two from the City of Bridgetown. In 1971, the system of single member constituencies was introduced, when the island was divided into 24 electoral districts, known as constituencies, each returning one member to Parliament. The number of constituencies was increased to 27 by the Representation of the People (Amendment) Act 1980 and further increased to 28 in 1990 and 30 in 2003. Single member constituencies offer a more equitable method of representation, since some effort is made to place approximately the same number of inhabitants in each constituency. Under the double member constituencies, some parishes contained many more inhabitants than others but returned the same two members to Parliament.

In the House of Assembly, the party which forms the Government normally sits to the right of the Speaker. The ministers sit in the front row and are referred to as members of the "front bench". They are the chief spokesmen for the Government and defend its policy in

Parliament. The other elected members of the ruling party are called "back benchers". It is possible that some members of the majority party in the House of Assembly may disagree with the Prime Minister or the policy of the party and refuse to vote in support of the party's programme in Parliament. If, at any time, the Prime Minister finds that he is unable to get the support of the majority of members of the House of Assembly, he has to resign or request the Governor-General to call an election.

From among the minority party or parties, the Governor-General appoints, as Leader of the Opposition, the person who is best able to command the support of the majority of those Members in Parliament who do not support the Government. In practice, this is usually the leader of the principal opposition party. If the Leader of the Opposition loses the support of the majority of opposition members of Parliament, he must resign or he will be removed from the office of Leader of the Opposition. In 1986, the leader of the Barbados Labour Party (BLP) was appointed Leader of the Opposition following a general election. In 1988, four members of the ruling Democratic Labour Party resigned from the party and formed the National Democratic Party (NDP). At that time, there were only three BLP members in Parliament. The leader of the NDP was, therefore, appointed Leader of the Opposition.

Specific functions are prescribed by the Constitution for the Leader of the Opposition. He has the right to nominate two members to sit in the Senate and he has to be consulted by the Prime Minister before some appointments, such as that of chief justice, are made.

Some of the members of the Opposition are their party's principal spokesmen on certain aspects of government and are known as "shadow" ministers. They are the persons most likely to form the Cabinet if their party should assume power and usually occupy the front row of the opposition seats.

In our system of government, it is important to have a strong Opposition, because this keeps the Government in check, since it knows there is a party prepared to provide the country with an alternative government, if the present Government acts contrary to the will of the majority of persons in the country. In addition, during an effective debate, the Opposition shows up the weakness in the Government's policy and generally serves as a reminder to the Government that there is a group which will make the country aware of any laws which are about to be passed, or any policy which is about to be adopted to the detriment of the country. The Opposition is an institution recognized by the Constitution and is sometimes referred to as "Her Majesty's Loyal Opposition".

It is sometimes argued that the two party system is inappropriate for small societies such as the Caribbean states since persons of obvious ability are deprived of making a contribution when their party is not in power. Those who advance this argument claim that there should be only one political party in the country, so that all the available talent could be used for the development of the people.

There is truth in the statement that able people are excluded from government under the two party system, but the experience of some countries which have a one-party system shows that the criterion for inclusion in the decision-making process is not necessarily ability, but unswerving loyalty to the party leadership. As a result, many able but independent persons are excluded because they do not put party loyalty before all other considerations. In addition, the choice of the public in selecting and changing their representatives is greatly reduced if not altogether removed.

Another argument in support of the one-party state is that politicians talk about democracy and people's rights when they are in opposition but when they assume power they act in a completely different way. Very often, policy and the programmes, which they criticized most while in opposition remain unchanged when they form the Government. It must be conceded that this type of opportunism exists, but it is submitted that this, in itself, is not good enough justification for changing our multi-party system.

Before the Lower House of Assembly meets, the list of matters to be discussed is prepared by the Clerk of Parliament and dispatched to the parliamentarians. The list which is really the agenda is called the Order Paper. If a back bencher or member of the Opposition wants to bring a resolution to Parliament, he drafts it and takes it to the Clerk of Parliament, who checks to see that it is written in parliamentary language and that it does not infringe any rules of Parliament; for example, if the resolution contains any provisions for the expenditure of public funds it will not be accepted, for only a minister of government can bring such a resolution. If the Member of Parliament cannot draft his own resolution, the Clerk of Parliament would give him assistance.

The Lower House is presided over by the Speaker who is elected at the beginning of each new Parliament. He does not normally take part in the debates and only votes if there is a tie. The Speaker is responsible for seeing that the rules on procedure, which are called standing orders, are followed and that all, including members of the Opposition, are treated fairly. The Speaker should, therefore, be someone in whom all Members of Parliament have confidence. It is also the duty of the Speaker to certify which bills are "money bills."

Sometimes the Members of Parliament vote to divert from the regular procedure laid down in the standing orders; for example, they may wish to change the order in which the business of the House is to be conducted – this diversion is referred to as "Suspension of the Standing Orders". When the House is meeting in committee, the Chairman of Committees, another elected member of the House, presides.

A minister usually introduces the matters to be debated. This is followed by speeches from members of either side of the House. After they have made their contribution, the minister is allowed to speak again to close the debate. Sometimes a bill is introduced by a back-bencher or a member of the Opposition. This is known as a 'private member's bill'.

During each meeting of Parliament, a time called "Question Time" is set aside when members of the House of Assembly, who are not members of the Cabinet, ask questions of ministers. The ministers either reply verbally or promise a written reply which is given at a later date.

Certain rules have to be observed in parliamentary debate; for example, all comments must be addressed to the Speaker or Chairman of Committees, and only one person may stand to speak at a time. Members are not permitted to call one another by name, but must refer to each other as the member for the constituency which he represents. If a member makes any derogatory remark about a fellow parliamentarian, he is called upon by the presiding officer to withdraw it and if he does not, he may be suspended.

At the end of the debate on a matter, the vote is taken. The Speaker asks those in favour to say "aye" and those against to say "no". After the members reply he announces, "The ayes have it", if the motion is passed, or "The noes have it", if the motion is rejected. There is not usually any need to count the votes since members of each party normally vote the same way. Sometimes, however, a member may call "divide"; the clerk then calls each member's name and records his "aye" or "no". At the completion of this, the Speaker announces the result.

To ensure that the people's representatives have complete freedom of speech, no legal action can be taken against Members of Parliament for anything which they say in Parliament. As a result, sometimes the members make statements in Parliament which, if made elsewhere, would be the subject of a lawsuit for defamation. It is sometimes thought that this protection given to parliamentarians is too great and is often abused. In deciding whether parliamentarians should continue to enjoy this complete freedom of speech we have to weigh the need to guarantee freedom of speech, against the need to protect other people's character. Parliamentarians should so conduct themselves that there would be no public clamour for a curb on the freedom of speech which they enjoy in pursuing the nation's business. This absolute freedom of speech is known as parliamentary immunity.

The symbol of authority in the House of Assembly is the 'mace'. This is a staff usually made of wood and metal, with a crown at the head. At the beginning of each sitting of the House of Assembly, the

Marshal bearing the mace escorts the Speaker into the House and places the mace in position, on a table in front of the Speaker. When the House is sitting in committee, the mace is moved from its position in front of the Speaker. At the end of a sitting of the House, the Marshal, bearing the mace, escorts the Speaker out of the Chamber. No business transacted in the House of Assembly is legal unless the mace is in its correct position. Some years ago, a member of the House of Assembly who wanted to express his disapproval of what was happening, grabbed the mace and removed it from its place. No further business could then be transacted until it was replaced.

The Senate

The function of the Senate is somewhat similar to that of the House of Lords in the British Parliament. One major difference is that no member of the Senate inherits his seat in the Chamber as is the case with many of the Lords in the British Upper House.

The Senate comprises 21 members – seven appointed by the Governor-General in his own discretion, 12 appointed by the Governor-General on the advice of the Prime Minister, and two appointed by the Governor-General on the advice of the Leader of the Opposition. The Senate conducts its business similarly to the House of Assembly. Instead of a Speaker, the Senate is presided over by its President, who is elected at the first meeting of the Chamber. If he is absent, his deputy takes the chair. The Upper House re-examines legislation passed in the House of Assembly and sometimes makes amendments to bills. Since Government has a majority in the Senate, all bills agreed on by the Cabinet usually pass through the Senate no matter how many opposition or independent senators may criticize it. For this reason, some people argue that the Senate should be abolished.

One of the arguments used by those who support the retention of the Senate is that it provides the Government with access to the expertise of a number of able persons who, for one reason or another, may have no interest in contesting a national election. The Governor-General, in his choice of candidates for the Senate, attempts to see that various interests, for example, religion, business and the law are represented. If there were no Upper House, some of these interests might not be represented in Parliament. Consideration should be given to a review of the Constitution to make provision for the Senate to become a more effective organ of government. Both the Government and the Opposition sometimes nominate persons who were unsuccessful in the election to be appointed to the Senate. It may be argued that this should not be done, since it may be interpreted as an attempt by a political leader, to reverse the decision of the electorate.

Members of the public are permitted to visit the Houses of Parliament and listen to the debates, but they may not interrupt members or misconduct themselves. If a Member of Parliament makes any reference to people in the public galleries who are listening to the debates, he refers to them as "strangers". The Speaker may order "strangers" to leave the House at anytime. It is hoped, however, that in a democratic country such as Barbados this right will not be exercised often, for citizens should be given every opportunity to see their representatives at work. With the widespread use of radio and television today, some parliamentary debates are now broadcast live. One effect this could have is to encourage a high standard of debates, for the members would be aware that their constituents are hearing and watching their conduct.

EXERCISES

1. (a) Name three rights that are enshrined in the Constitution.

   (b) Can you think of any other rights which are not in the present Constitution, but which should have been included?

2. (a) How is the Prime Minister chosen?

   (b) What are the functions of the Leader of the Opposition?

   (c) Should the Governor-General always accept the advice of the Prime Minister, even when he is exercising the functions which the Constitution provided to be exercised after consultation with (and not on the advice of) the Prime Minister?

   (d) What are the advantages and disadvantages of a Republican form of government?

3. Explain the following terms:
   (a) The franchise   (b) Adult suffrage
   (c) Democracy   (d) The Cabinet
   (e) Republic   (f) Referendum

4. Discuss and debate the following topics.

   (a) "A one-party system of government is the best form of government for Barbados"

   (b) "Voluntarily Idle" persons should not be permitted to vote at general elections."

   (c) "The retention of the Queen of England as the head of state of Barbados is not in keeping with the political independence of the country."

   (d) "Anyone found guilty of plotting against the duly elected government should be deprived of his citizenship."

THINGS TO DO

5. Find out which Commonwealth Caribbean countries are republics and which are constitutional monarchies.

6. Pay a visit to Parliament and ask to see an Order Paper; then organize a parliament to debate a motion to amend the Barbados Constitution to remove the right to own private property.

7. Abraham Lincoln made a famous speech on democracy at Gettysburg. Find the text of this speech and state why you consider it important.

8. "The move towards a republican form of government is a necessary step for a maturing and independent nation." Discuss.

CHAPTER 5

THE LAWS OF THE LAND

"Even when laws have been written down, they ought not always to remain unaltered."

Aristotle (384-322 B.C.)

Law As An Instrument of Social Change

The laws of Barbados are enacted by Parliament. Law can be an instrument of social advancement or a means of repression. It is precisely because laws can be employed to undermine the interest of a society that citizens ought to keep abreast of changes in legislation. As an instrument of social progress, legislation sets the framework within which the society develops. For example, prior to the 1930s, there existed in the statute books, laws which made trade unions illegal. Today, those laws have been replaced by laws which not only legalize trade unions, but which protect the rights of workers. Some of these include The Severance Payment Act Chapter 355, Protection of Wages Act Chapter 351, Holiday with Pay Act Chapter 348, and the Employment of Women (Maternity Leave) Act, Chapter 345A. The various segregation laws enacted by the South African Government in the 1960s to ensure separation between whites and blacks and to perpetuate exploitation represent an excellent example of repressive legislation.

Before a new law is passed, instructions for its drafting are given to the legal draughtsmen to put into legislative form. Often the draft is circulated among persons who have a particular interest in the legislation, for their comments. Labour legislation, for example, would normally be sent to both employer and employee organizations. Some important proposed legislation is even circulated for the general public to express their views on it. After the Cabinet has accepted the final draft, the piece of legislation is then taken to Parliament to go through the various stages necessary for it to become law. The practice of acquainting interested bodies of proposed legislation should be encouraged in a democracy, for it gives the citizen an opportunity to express his views on legislation which will affect him. Sometimes as a result of public protest, some unpopular proposals are withdrawn before they are enacted by Parliament.

Draft legislation before it reaches the statute book is called a bill. Although bills (other than money bills) can be introduced in either the House of Assembly or the Senate, the majority of bills are introduced in the House of Assembly. Any bill which involves the expenditure of public money must originate in the House of Assembly, since it is felt that the elected representatives of the people are the correct persons to decide on the spending of public funds.

The bill is first placed before the House to be introduced to the members; this is known as the first reading. At this stage there is no debate on the bill. Next, it is printed and the general principles are debated. This stage which is known as the second reading is an important stage, for it is here that the merits of the bill are outlined by those proposing it, while the shortcomings are shown up by its opponents. After this stage comes the committee stage when the bill is discussed clause by clause and any necessary amendments are made. The bill is then reported back to the House (report stage) for the third reading, after which it is accepted or rejected as a whole, but there are no amendments at this stage.

After the bill has been accepted by the House of Assembly, it is sent to the Senate, where the same procedure is followed, and at the end of the third reading in the Senate, it is sent to the Governor-General for his assent and becomes law.

To ensure that the real power of government remains in the hands of the elected members of the House of Assembly, the Constitution provides that any measure other than the amendment to the Constitution, passed by the House of Assembly, can become a law without the assent of the Senate. If a money bill is passed by the House of Assembly and sent to the Senate at least a month before the end of the session and it is not passed by the Senate, it may be presented to the Governor-General for his assent without the consent of the Senate. In the case of a bill other than a money bill if it is passed by the House of Assembly in two successive sessions, at least one month before the end of each session, and is rejected by the Senate in each session, it may be presented to the Governor-General for his assent, without the approval of the Senate, provided at least seven months have elapsed between the passing of the Bill by the House of Assembly in the first session and second sessions.

It is recognized that the elected government has the right to pass laws for the governance of the country, however. the Constitution provides certain safeguards to protect the citizen from the tyranny of an unscrupulous government. One such safeguard is that the responsibility for interpreting the laws is placed on the law courts and not on Parliament itself. After a law has been passed, therefore, if there is any question as to its real meaning, the law courts have to decide on the correct interpretation of that law. As we have seen earlier, the courts can even find that a particular law is unconstitutional, and thus declare it null and void.

The Courts
"Justice is truth in Action." Disraeli (1804-1881)

One of the basic requirements of any civilized community is a system of justice in which the citizen has confidence. If there is not some recognized way in which to resolve our differences, we could most likely adopt the rule of the jungle that might is right.

In Barbados, we have inherited our system of justice from the British. Two important features of this system are that all persons are equal before the law; this principle is commonly known as the Rule of Law. The other feature is that every citizen accused of a crime is considered innocent until he is proven guilty in a competent court of law.

The courts at all levels exercise both criminal and civil jurisdiction. Generally, the criminal courts deal with cases which are brought against the citizen at the instance of the State, while the civil courts hear cases brought by one citizen against another or a citizen against the State. For example, if someone is accused of robbing another person and he is taken before the court, the offence with which he is charged is a criminal matter. If on the other hand, two persons entered into a contract and one of the parties did not carry out his part of the bargain, any redress sought from the courts would be a civil matter.

There are three levels in the court system; at the top is the Caribbean Court of Justice which is the final court of appeal for Barbados. This court is also the final court of appeal for Guyana, and it is expected that eventually it will become the final court of appeal for some other Caribbean countries.

Next is the Supreme Court of Judicature which comprises the Court of Appeal and the High Court. The Chief Justice is the head of the Judiciary; he is also the President of the Court of Appeal. Beside the Chief Justice there are four other judges called Justices of Appeal who comprise the Court of Appeal. This court is an appellate court and hears appeals from the High Court and the Magistrates' Courts. In criminal matters, the Court of Appeal hears appeals against the conviction or against the sentence imposed upon an offender at trial. In civil cases, the court hears appeals against the decision of the judge or the magistrate. On the hearing of an appeal, the court has wide powers. It may confirm, reverse or vary the decision of the lower court or remit the case for hearing on a particular point to the lower court.

The High Court hears the more serious civil and criminal matters. The judges of the High Court were formerly called puisne judges, but are now referred to as judges of the High Court. The High Court consists of eight High Court judges. There are three divisions of the High Court: The Civil Division, the Family Division and the Criminal Division.

The Civil Division of the High Court is concerned with the more important civil matters such as disputes over land, wills, breach of contract and other civil disputes. The Family Division is concerned with divorces, matters relating to children including maintenance and disputes over custody and division of marital property. The Criminal Division hears serious offences, such as murder, rape and arson. Offences of this nature are know *indictable offences* and are tried before a judge and jury.

At the base of the system are the magistrates' courts which deal with minor criminal offences known as summary offences. They also hold preliminary enquiries into serious criminal offences and hear minor civil matters. These courts are presided over by magistrates. Barbados is divided into six magisterial districts, A, B, C, D, E and F to hear matters committed in the respective districts. For administrative purposes, sometimes a magistrate's court such as the Traffic Court, the Juvenile Court and the Coroner's Court may deal with specialized matters.

The Coroner's Court

In the Coroner's Court, the magistrate sits as coroner to enquire into violent, unnatural suspicious deaths and into the circumstances where a person died while in police custody, in prison or as a result of injury caused by a police officer in the execution of his duty. The holding of an inquest in such circumstances is mandatory. This court is serviced by a magistrate who conducts the inquest. The object of the inquest is to enquire into the cause of death of the deceased to determine whether any person is criminally liable for the death.

The Traffic Court

The Traffic Court is concerned with the hearing of minor road traffic offences such as exceeding the speed limit.

The Juvenile Court

The Juvenile Court hears matters concerning criminal charges against children and young persons. Such persons are between the ages of 11 and 16 years. Proceedings in this court are less formal than in other Magistrates' Courts and are often closed to the public, as well as to members of the media. Only the members and officers of the court, the parties to the case, their attorneys-at-law and other persons directly concerned in the case, are allowed to be in attendance. The magistrate may summon or issue a warrant for the parents of the child or young person to attend court. Only by special order of the court will representatives of a newspaper or news agency be allowed to be present during proceedings in this court. It is an offence for persons to publish the name, address, school and photograph or anything likely to lead to the identification of the child or young person before the Juvenile Court. Upon hearing the case, the magistrate has power to sentence the child, order corporal punishment, impose a fine on the child and his parent, grant an absolute discharge, and make a probation order or an order of remand to a reformatory and industrial school.

The Procedure in the Magistrates' Court

Trial in the Magistrates' Court as in the High Court is held in 'open court'. However, the magistrate may decide to clear the court room for special reasons. In such cases, the matter is heard in camera". Such situations will usually arise in cases involving sexual offences or juveniles.

In the Magistrate's Court there is a case list from which all matters to he heard are called. The court sits at 9:00 a.m. and the complainant, the person who brings the charge, and the defendant, the person

THE ORGANIZATION OF THE LAW COURTS IN BARBADOS

The Caribbean Court of Justice (CCJ)
The final appellate court

Court of Appeal (CA)

High Court (HC)

Criminal Division	Civil Division	Family Division

Magistrates' Courts

Criminal Court	Traffic Court	Juvenile Court	Coroner's Court	Civil Court

against whom the charge is brought, are both expected to be present for the hearing. In addition, witnesses who are summoned to Court must also attend. If both the complainant and defendant appear the magistrate may proceed to hear the case. However, if the complainant fails to appear or neither party appears, the magistrate may dismiss the case or adjourn it for another date of hearing.

When a person is accused of an indictable offence, there is a preliminary enquiry by a magistrate, who determines whether there is enough evidence to justify the case going before the High Court for trial.

If such a case is made out, the matter then goes to the High Court where it is tried before a judge and jury. The assizes at which these cases were tried previously were held four times each year, in January, April, July and October. However, from April of 2006 criminal trials are held continuously during the year, except in August, during the court's vacation.

During criminal trials, the judge directs the jury on matters of law, but they alone are the sole judges of fact. In trials on indictment for murder and treason, the jury consists of 12 jurors and in trials on indictment for any other criminal matter, the jury consists of nine jurors.

The Jury

The jury system has for a long time been one of the cornerstones of our legal system. The notion that a man is entitled to be tried by a jury of his peers has been a feature of the English Law since the 1880s. Persons should, therefore, consider it a special honour to be selected for jury service. It is the civil duty of every person who is selected to attend court and carry out his duties faithfully and with the highest integrity. It is an offence punishable by fine, for a person selected for duty to refuse to serve without reasonable cause.

Persons may be summoned by the Registrar of the Supreme Court from among the names appearing in the Jurors' book. This book is prepared on a national basis and comprises randomly selected names from the electoral register. The number of jurors summoned by the registrar for jury service is within the registrar's discretion. He may summon as many persons as are necessary for the business of the court.

Qualifications for Jury Service

Eligibility for jury service is governed by the Juries Act Chapter 115B. A person is qualified to serve as a juror and liable to attend for jury service if:

(a)   he is a citizen of Barbados who is ordinarily resident in Barbados;

(b)   he is over the age of 18 years and under the age of 65 years; and

(c)   he is literate.

However, persons who fall into this category may nonetheless be disqualified from service if they:

(a)   have been convicted of any criminal offence and have been sentenced to imprisonment;

(b)   are persons of unsound mind;

(c)   are deaf or blind;

(d)   are declared bankrupt under the laws of Barbados and are still bankrupt;

(e)   have entered into a deed of arrangement with their creditors.

Exemptions from Jury Service

Certain persons, although not ineligible for jury service, if asked to serve, can claim to he excused as of right from service; they include:

(a)   members and officers of the Senate or House of Assembly;

(b)   judges;

(c)   magistrates;

(d)   ministers of the Christian religion;

(e)   heads of, and members of missions;

(f)   members of the armed forces of the Crown;

(g)   members of the police force:

(h)   attorneys-at-law;

(i)   legally qualified medical practitioners;

(j)   wife or husband of persons mentioned above.

Discretionary Excusal

The act also provides that the court may excuse anyone from service because of physical disability or insufficient understanding of the English language, or if he can show a good cause or reason to be excused from service.

Selection of the Jury

At trial, the names of jurors to be empanelled to hear a particular case are selected by ballot by the court clerk. On selection each person goes into the jury box to he sworn. Before the jury is sworn, the accused is entitled to challenge up to nine persons without giving any reason for the challenge. He may also challenge any member for cause. For example, if the accused is Jewish, and the potential juror is a known anti-Semitic, that juror can be challenged for cause.

The Prosecution may also challenge for cause. In addition they have a right of challenge without cause, under a procedure known as the "stand-by" procedure. The prosecution may on behalf of the Crown call upon a potential juror to "stand by" that is, to be excluded from the jury unless it is impossible for the jury to be empanelled without calling this juror. In practice that juror is not called again.

The persons who are not challenged are then sworn or affirmed if the taking of an oath is against their religious beliefs. The jury is then addressed by the court clerk, who reads the charge against the accused to them. The clerk then informs them that at the conclusion of the case, after hearing all the evidence, they must return a true verdict of not guilty or guilty against the accused.

Legal Aid

In criminal cases where the penalty is death or where the offence is very serious, such as rape, in an effort to ensure that the accused is not denied justice on account of his poverty, the Crown provides an attorney-at-law to defend him if he is unable to afford one. The Community Legal Services Act Chapter 112A, makes provision for legal aid to be given in a number of other matters including family matters, and all indictable offences where the accused is a minor. legal aid is a system of free legal services to people of insufficient means.

At this stage of our development, the services of a lawyer should be available to any citizen who is in need of legal advice. Legal aid should, therefore, be extended to accused persons in all criminal cases and to needy persons in most civil and family matters.

The Judiciary

Our judges have long been known for their integrity and impartiality. This reputation inspires confidence in our judicial system and should always be maintained. In order to preserve the independence of the judiciary from any interference, the Constitution provides certain safeguards for the security of tenure of the judges. They are also protected from any legal action being taken against them far anything which they say or do during a trial.

The chief justice and other judges are appointed by the Governor-General on the advice of the Prime Minister, after consultation with the Leader of the Opposition. Once they have been appointed, however, there can be no political interference with the manner in which they perform their duties. Their salary cannot he reduced while they hold office, neither can they be dismissed except for misconduct or inability to perform their duties.

Some Officers of The Court

By the introduction of the Legal Profession Act in 1973, all legal practitioners in Barbados are styled attorneys-at-law. Previously there were solicitors and barristers-at-law, the Solicitors used to concentrate mainly on office work like conveyancing and the drawing up of other documents, while the barristers were those who would appear in court as advocates. Since 1973 there has been a fusion of the two branches of the profession.

Some senior attorneys-at-law who have been admitted to the Bar for not less than 10 years are accorded the honour and dignity of being Queen's Counsel. These appointments are made by the Governor-General on the recommendation of the Prime Minister, after consultation with the chief justice and the Bar Association.

Qualifications of an Attorney-at-Law

In order to become an attorney-at-law one must be the holder of an LL.B. degree from the University of the West Indies (UWI) or from the University of Guyana or a law degree equivalent to the UWI LL.B., from a university approved by the Council of Legal Education. After completion of the LL.B. degree prospective attorneys must acquire the Legal Education Certificate awarded by the Council of Legal Education. In order to receive the Legal Education Certificate, a person must have studied for two years at one of the region's law schools situated in Trinidad, Jamaica or The Bahamas. Persons who have been admitted to the bar of a common law country may also he admitted to practise in Barbados provided they completed a further six months period of training at one of the region's law schools.

All persons admitted to practise law in Barbados need to have a valid practising certificate. A practising certificate is issued on an annual basis to an attorney-at-law whose name is on the Roll of Attorneys and who has paid his annual fees to the Registration Department and the Bar Association. Any attorney-at-law who practises or conducts business without a valid practising certificate commits an offence and is subject to disciplinary action.

The Attorney-General

The attorney-general is the principal legal advisor to the Government. He is a minister of government appointed by the Prime Minister and is a member of the Cabinet. The attorney-general does not normally take any part in criminal proceedings; this is the work of the director of public prosecutions and his staff who prosecute on behalf of the Crown.

The Director of Public Prosecutions

It is the Director of Public Prosecutions who decides whether legal proceedings should be instituted or whether an action which has started should be discontinued. Like the judges his security of tenure is guaranteed by the Constitution. Since 1974 after an amendment to the Constitution, the Attorney-General has the power to give directions to the Director of Public Prosecutions on matters which are political or which deal with international affairs.

The Solicitor-General

The solicitor-general is subordinate to the attorney-general. He is appointed to office by the Governor-General, acting on the recommendation of the Judicial and Legal Service Commission, after that commission has consulted the Prime Minister. He is the attorney-general's principal legal advisor in civil matters involving the Crown.

The Registrar of the Supreme Court

The Registrar is responsible for the administration of the Supreme Court. His functions and responsibilities are governed by the Supreme Court of Judicature Act Chapter 11 7A. The Registrar has the authority and powers to hear and decide certain specified judicial proceedings. These include application for judgment in default and for Summons for Directions. His duties also include having custody of the seal of the Court of Appeal and of the High Court and of all documents, records and papers of the courts.

Justices of the Peace

In most communities in Barbados, there is a justice of the peace (JP), who is available to offer his or her services to the community.

A JP ought to be a person of unquestionable integrity who seeks to provide and protect the rights of the individual in a particular community.

Justices of the peace are appointed by a warrant issued by the Governor-General on the advice of the Prime Minister. Before assuming responsibilities as a JP, the individual is required to take the Oath of Allegiance and the Judicial Oath.

A person who is appointed JP is usually a mature individual who commands the respect and confidence of members of his community.

There is a special category of persons who are justices of the peace by virtue of their office. These include:

(a)   magistrates;

(b)   The Commissioner of Police and some senior police officers;

(c)   The superintendent of the prisons;

(d)   the chief immigration officer;

(e)   the private secretary of the Governor-General;

(f)   The registrar and deputy registrars.

Justices of the peace have several functions conferred upon them by law.

The Police

We have seen how the machinery of justice works, but the maintenance of law and order, and the administration of justice would not have been possible if there were no organization to ensure that everybody obeys the law of the land or are punished for not doing so.

Unfortunately, all members of society do not allow their love for their country and their concern for their fellow men to govern their behaviour, so it becomes necessary for the force of authority to be used against them. It is the police on which we have to depend to perform this duty.

As early as 1835, Barbados had an established police force. Without such a force there would most likely be complete chaos in our society: the strong and selfish would enjoy their life at the expense of the weak. It is the police force on which we must depend to help safeguard our rights and preserve law and order. We should, therefore, not regard the police as enemies or oppressors, but rather as friends and protectors. Members of the police force are not employed merely to apprehend those persons who commit crimes, but they have the much more positive and important function of crime prevention.

In former times, much of the strength of the police lay in the use of force. Law enforcement officers would he appointed, therefore, partly because of their brawn, but today things have changed; the police force has been able to attract more educated young men and women who are equipped to carry out scientific investigation of crime and who are exposed to sociological studies of the community which they serve.

Members of the police force are trained at the Regional Police Training School in various disciplines including elementary law, police procedures, weapons training and self-defence. After this initial training, some members of the police force further their studies in law and other academic subjects. It is the duty of all citizens to do everything in their power to maintain our reputation of being a law abiding nation.

The police force is supplemented by a Permanent Special Constabulary. The Special Constabulary is under the command of the Commissioner of Police. Special Constables are vested with all the powers, authority, privileges, immunities and responsibilities of a member of the police force.

Police Band

The Barbados Police Band, which is an arm of the local police force, provides music for entertainment of thousands at home and abroad. It has been acclaimed internationally for its performances.

The band of the Royal Barbados Police Force was established in 1889 with a complement of 19 serving policemen, whose common interests were a love for music and knowledge of the arts. At that time, they wore regulation uniforms for their performances. The band has toured extensively overseas since their first tour in St. Lucia in 1945. They became the first military hand to broadcast via satellite while on the Ed Sullivan Show in 1962. They have performed and received standing ovations at the Edinburgh Tattoo in Scotland; Disney World, Florida: Music of the Nations, Germany; Earls Court, London; Radio City (USA) and throughout the Caribbean.

EXERCISES

1. Describe the stages through which a bill passes before being passed into law.

2. *(a)* Is wide consultation desirable before a bill becomes law?
   (b) How is such consultation carried out?

3. *(a)* What is the role of the Senate in the law-making process?
   (b) Can you think of changes to the composition or functions of the Senate that would make it more effective?

4. What suggestions would you make to improve the law-making function of the Senate?

5. In what court would you expect the following cases to be tried?
   (a) John Brown is suing his former employers for wrongful dismissal.
   (b) Mary Jones is seeking support from Tom Jones for her infant child.
   (c) Jim stole a radiogram from his neighbour's house and was arrested by the police.

6. What is the meaning of C.I.D? Explain the function of that body.

7. Explain the following:
   (a) arson
   (b) manslaughter
   (c) nolle prosequi

8. *(a)* What are the functions of a Coroner's Court?
   (b) What is a court of original jurisdiction?
   (c) What are the advantages and disadvantages of the CCJ replacing the Privy Council as the final court of appeal for the Caribbean countries?

9. Debate: "The jury system ought to be abolished."

10. Which of the following is correct? A person charged with manslaughter is tried by:
    (a) two judges.
    (b) a judge and jury.
    (c) a single judge.
    (d) a jury of 12 persons.

THINGS TO DO

11. Pay a visit to the court; observe the procedure, then organize a mock trial.

CHAPTER 6
PUBLIC OFFICERS

"Public Officers are the servants and agents of the people to execute the laws which the people hate made."

Grover Cleveland (1837-1908)

The Civil Service

Ministers of government are chosen either from those persons who have been elected to Parliament by the people, or are appointed by the Prime Minister in his capacity as the leader of the elected representatives of the people. They have the overall responsibility for the various government departments which come under their ministry and give the political directives for their functioning. However, the day-to-day planning, supervising and policy implementation are the responsibility of a body of workers known as civil servants.

Traditionally, the civil service is an organization of full-time employees who provide continuous service to the public, no matter what government is in power. Senior civil servants are expected to give the elected government the best advice at their disposal and all civil servants have the duty to carry out faithfully the policy of the elected government provided it is not illegal, whether they agree with it or not. If a civil servant finds that he cannot, in conscience carry out the policy of the duly elected government, he is expected to resign rather than work against it. Since civil servants are supposed to be impartial and carry out the policies of whichever party is elected to form the Government they are not allowed to take an active part in politics by speaking on political platforms or writing to the press on political matters.

They may, however, join political parties and, of course, they can exercise their constitutional right to vote in elections.

Civil servants are appointed by the Governor-General on the advice of an impartial body known as the Public Service Commission and are disciplined and dismissed by that body. For those civil servants who hold a job which requires a legal qualification, the body in charge of their appointment, discipline and dismissal is the Judicial and Legal Service Commission, while the Police Service Commission deals with matters of appointments etc. relating to police officers.

The reason for instituting an impartial body to make appointments to the Public Service is to avoid political interference or the bringing of other pressures to influence the appointment of such officers. However, permanent secretaries, who are the heads of ministries and who have to work very closely with the ministers, as well as deputy permanent secretaries, heads and deputy heads of departments are appointed by the Governor-General on the recommendation of the appropriate Service Commission after consultation with the Prime Minister. Members of the foreign service are also appointed on the recommendation of the Prime Minister.

The Constitution provides safeguards for the security of tenure of certain civil servants, the chief of these being the Director of Public Prosecutions and the Auditor-General. Because of the importance of the function of these officers and the serious consequences which can result to the society if they are vulnerable to the pressures of unscrupulous persons, every effort has to be made to ensure that they are not influenced in the performance of their duties by special interests or other pressures.

Consequently, there are special procedures laid down in the Constitution for the dismissal of these officers. The Constitution also provides that their salary cannot he reduced during their term of office. This provision prevents any indirect method of getting rid of these officers in circumstances where they could not be otherwise dismissed.

As was stated earlier the Director of Public Prosecutions has the sole responsibility to initiate, continue or discontinue criminal prosecutions in all cases other than those which involve security and international affairs, where he is subject to the direction of the Attorney-General, a politically appointed officer. These exceptions were introduced in the constitutional amendments of 1974. The Auditor-General has the important duty of seeing that public funds are not misappropriated. He is required to lay a report in Parliament annually. In this report, any shortcomings in the manner in which a government department has managed its financial affairs are highlighted.

The conditions of service of all other public officers and employees are governed by the *General Orders for the Public Service of Barbados 1970*. These orders govern matters pertaining to the appointment and transfer of public servants, the disciplinary procedures to be followed in dealing with a public servant, the salaries and allowances they are to be paid and their pensions and gratuities.

Divisions of the Civil Service

There are six main categories in the Barbados Civil Service.

1. Administrative – In this category are found the main advisers to the Minister headed by the permanent secretary. This group comprises the senior administrative officers. The permanent Secretary is the administrative head of each ministry and all advice to the minister goes through him. He is responsible not only for advising the minister as to alternatives available on various matters, but also to see that decisions of the minister and the Cabinet are executed.

2. Professional – These are persons with specialist qualifications who are employed to offer specialized advice in their various disciplines. This group includes accountants, medical doctors, engineers and lawyers.

3. Technical – This group of employees is semi-professional. They use their technical skill for the implementation of government programmes.

4. Executive – After the decisions have been made by the minister generally on the advice of the administrative and professional staff, an executive group is responsible for the day-to-day execution of the policy within the framework laid down.

5. Clerical and stenographic – This group comprises clerks, typists, machine operators, receptionists, etc. It plays a supportive role to those mentioned above.

6. General workers – messengers, office attendants, cleaners, maids, watchmen, and other subordinate staff. All these workers contribute in various ways to the efficient functioning of government departments.

Government Ministries and Departments

It is the Prime Minister who decides which subjects form the portfolio of each minister. Each minister is responsible for the overall policy of the departments of Government that are in his ministry. The combination of departments for which a minister may be responsible may vary from time to time even during the term of office of a particular minister. For example, in some governments, information forms part of the portfolio of the Prime Minister, and the Minister of Education is responsible for culture. In some other administrations, there is a

Minister of Information and Culture. The Minister of Health was at one time responsible for national insurance; at another time, this department was part of the portfolio of the Minister of Labour and National Insurance.

Whichever minister has the political responsibility for a department, however, the general function of the department remains the same.

Now, we will look at the functions of some ministries and government departments.

Ministry of Education, Youth Affairs and Sports

Over the years, Barbados has boasted of an exceptionally high rate of literacy. This situation has developed out of the work of the Church and successive governments.

Soon after the English settlers came to Barbados, they established educational institutions for their children, and after emancipation, other institutions were established for the instruction of the descendants of the freed slaves.

As early as 1745, Barbados had the first institution of higher learning to be established in a British Colony, when Codrington College, an affiliate of the University of Durham was opened in St. John.

Successive governments have continued to place great emphasis on education; a major portion of the government's budget is spent on education. Today, education for Barbadian citizens at all levels from kindergarten to University is financed by the taxpayers of Barbados. The Ministry of Education is responsible for the administration of the entire educational system other than at university level. At the head of the ministry is the permanent secretary, who is the chief administrative officer, and the chief education officer, who is the principal professional officer. While the permanent secretary is concerned with the administrative aspects of the ministry, the chief education officer, who is an experienced educator, advises the minister on professional matters.

The educational system is divided into three broad categories:
(a) Primary *(b)* Secondary *(c)* Tertiary

Primary

At the primary stage, there are nursery schools and over 100 government primary schools. Recruitment to secondary education in public schools is through a common entrance examination. Like other aspects of our education, the Common Entrance Examination was adopted from the United Kingdom experience. Some argue that schoolchildren should proceed from the primary to secondary stage automatically, while others defend the system of competitive examinations. It is left for the Minister of Education, after considering the pros and cons, to make the final recommendations to Cabinet whether the present system should continue, if it should be abolished completely, or if it should undergo modification. In any case, the citizens through parent-teachers associations and other organizations should listen carefully to the debate, and after considering all the circumstances bring their own informed opinion to bear on the final outcome.

Secondary

There are 23 government secondary schools in Barbados. One sometimes hears of the older secondary schools and the newer secondary schools. The former, as the title suggests are those secondary schools which were established in the country in the earliest periods of secondary education. Harrison College, for example, was first opened in 1733. These older schools are traditional grammar school types. On the other hand, the first of the newer multi-lateral secondary schools was established in 1952.

Because of the historical development of these two types of schools, they were administered somewhat differently. The older schools were managed by governing bodies, which were virtually autonomous. On the other hand, the Ministry of Education exercised far greater control over the newer secondary schools. The Education Act 1981 provides for the control of all government secondary schools. There are now boards of management, which are accountable to the Ministry of Education. Among the functions of these boards of management is the recruitment of staff. Such appointments, however, have to be confirmed by the Ministry of Education and the appointments of school principals must be approved by the Cabinet.

There are also a number of private secondary schools. Those whose standards are approved by the Ministry of Education receive financial assistance from government.

Tertiary

This level includes institutions such as the Barbados Community College, Erdiston Teachers' Training College, the Samuel Jackman Prescod Polytechnic, which offers training in technical and vocational subjects. In addition, there is a branch of the University of the West Indies, at Cave Hill, which offers instruction in most academic and professional areas, including law and medicine.

Erdiston College

This is a co-educational institute for the training of teachers. It was established in 1948, under the Erdiston Teachers Training College, Board of Management Order.

The Community College

The Barbados Community College was established in 1968 by an Act of Parliament, the Barbados Community College Act 1968 – 23. This Act was amended in 1990 to empower the College to grant bachelor's degrees, associate degrees, diplomas and certificates to students who successfully complete approved programmes of study. The community college offers educational training in a wide range of subjects, including liberal arts, commerce, technology, science and fine arts.

The University of the West Indies

This regional institution is funded by and serves as the principal tertiary institution for 15 countries in the English-speaking Caribbean. It was founded in 1948 at the Mona campus in Jamaica, as a university college in a special relationship with the University of London. The university achieved independent status by charter in 1962.

There are three main campuses of the University. They are the Cave Hill campus in Barbados, the St. Augustine Campus in the Republic of Trinidad & Tobago and the Mona campus in Jamaica. There are 12 regional centres in other contributing countries which offer basic tuition.

The university curriculum offers a wide cross-section of disciplines including agriculture, engineering, the medical sciences, law, business, social sciences, nursing, communications, humanities and the natural sciences.

Other Educational Institutions

Although the school is of utmost importance, all education does not take place in the classroom. There are other educational institutions: these all came under the portfolio of the Minister of Education, but some have been transferred to other ministries. Among the other education institutions are The Barbados Public Library, which was founded in 1847, the Barbados Museum, and the Archives Department.

A visit to the Barbados Museum can be quite educational. In a short time, one is afforded the opportunity to compare the present and the past. The museum contains relics of slavery and the sugar industry, geographical and archeological specimens as well as typical furniture, cutlery and crockery of the old plantation days. There is also a collection of birds and fish that were found in and around Barbados.

At the Archives Department can be found old documents in which are recorded the history of our country. Among the interesting documents found in the archives are those dealing with the emancipation of the slaves, 18th-Century minutes of the House of Assembly and old newspapers printed in Barbados dating back to 1783.

All youths should make a special effort to become members of the public library and to visit other educational institutions.

In addition, this ministry has responsibility for the development of youth programmes in Barbados. To this end, it has established programmes which have been instrumental in the development of social, educational and other skills among the nation's youth. Some of these programmes include *the Barbados Youth Service, the Youth Development Programme, the Youth Entrepreneur Scheme and the Annual National Summer Camp Programme.*

National Insurance Office

The measures which a society introduces to take care of the poor and disabled are a good barometer of the society's conscience. Not many years ago, old and disabled persons who could not support themselves were placed in 'almshouses'. In a real sense, in these poor houses were to be found the forgotten ones. Inability to support oneself in one's old age was not necessarily caused by lack of foresight; we must remember that as late as the 1930s many workers were paid less than subsistence wages. It is, therefore, no cause for surprise that many persons were unable to save and ended up in the country's almshouses.

With the passage of time, measures were introduced to ameliorate the conditions of the poor and disabled. Prominent among such measures was the enactment in 1966 of national insurance legislation. National insurance is planned to replace the old-age pension scheme.

Under the scheme, all persons from 16 to 65 years are eligible for insurance and must register with the scheme if they are employed.

Every employer is bound by law to make specified deductions from his employees' earnings and is required to remit the money deducted with his own contribution to the National Insurance Office. In addition self-employed persons must register and contribute to the scheme.

The National Insurance Scheme provides various types of benefits to those insured. These include sickness, maternity, invalidity, and survivors' benefits, contributory old-age pensions, non-contributory old-age pensions, funeral grants and unemployment benefits.

Any person, who has been insured for at least 13 weeks and has paid in at least eight contributions in the 13 weeks immediately preceding the one in which he became ill, is eligible for sickness benefit for up to 26 weeks. In some cases, the period during which benefits will be paid is even longer.

In the case where the insured worker has become permanently incapacitated as a result of illness before reaching age 65, he is entitled to invalidity benefits either in the form of a lump sum payment or a pension, provided certain requirements are met. Insured persons who have reached age $65\frac{1}{2}$ and have paid a certain number of contributions are eligible for a pension. They may opt, however, to receive a reduced pension from age 62 or defer their pension until after $65\frac{1}{2}$, but not later than 67, in which case they would receive an increased pension.

The particular aspect of the National Insurance Scheme which recommends it is the shifting away of the measures from a category of a 'hand-out' to the destitute. National Insurance funds also provide a substantial source of funds for investment.

Ministry of Health

A substantial amount of government's annual recurrent expenditure is spent on health. The services include preventive and curative care, provided by a team of health workers attached to hospitals, health centres, polyclinics, the sanitation department and the public health engineering unit.

The chief administrative officer of the Ministry of Health is the permanent secretary, while the chief medical officer, a registered medical practitioner, is the chief technical adviser.

The Queen Elizabeth Hospital is the primary health care institution in Barbados. It was built in 1964 and has a complement of 600 beds. It provides medical, surgical, casualty and out-patient services. Specialist services are also provided; some of these are obstetrics, cardiac surgery, gynaecology, pediatrics and ophthalmology. This hospital is operated by a board of management and is funded primarily by the Government of Barbados. The Queen Elizabeth Hospital, which is one of the most up-to-date hospitals in the West Indies, is a teaching hospital and serves the Faculty of Medical Sciences of the University of the West Indies.

At Black Rock, St. Michael, there is a psychiatric hospital with 600 beds. It provides care for acute and chronic in-patients. There is also an out-patients clinic service and community follow-up programme.

This ministry also administers a number of district hospitals. These provide mainly geriatric services. The largest of these is the St. Michael Geriatric Hospital with over 350 beds.

Health centres and polyclinics, which provide social, preventive as well as limited curative services, are located in various parts of the island. The main health centres and polyclinics administer sub-clinics in all parishes. The care provided by these agencies serves to reduce the pressure on the hospitals, especially the Queen Elizabeth Hospital. These clinics also provide service reasonably near to the homes of persons who live in rural areas.

The Sanitation Services Authority is responsible for the collection and disposal of refuse and maintains the few remaining public baths.

The Public Health Engineering Unit and Public Health Inspectorate are concerned with a number of facilities some of which are protection of the island's ground water supply, surveillance and control of land, sea and atmosphere pollution as well as swimming pool maintenance and the quality control of food. In its effort to maintain an uncontaminated ground water supply, the Public Health Engineering Unit advises on land and building development. This necessitates the examination of proposals for sewage and industrial waste.

The Ministry of Social Transformation

The Ministry of Social Transformation was established in January 1999 in order to provide for the rationalization of social and welfare services and to alter the social environment of this country. The primary focus of this ministry is to provide aid to the poor, the disadvantaged and disabled of society. Among the functions of the ministry are:

1. The provision of assistance to vulnerable groups in society such as the elderly, children and the disabled.

2. The creation of policies for persons with disabilities.

3. Fostering of care for the elderly and those living under respite care.

The ministry is also responsible for a number of agencies including the following:

1. *The Child Care Board*: This agency is charged with the care and protection of the nation's children. Its duty is to ensure that any child who is in need of care and protection is taken into care, in a home, in which there exists stability and affection.

2. *The Bureau of Gender Affairs*: This agency is responsible for matters pertaining to gender development. It provides advice to government on gender affairs.

3. *The National Assistance Board*: The objective of this agency is to maintain the dignity of elderly persons in Barbados through the provision of social support and recreational services. Some of the services which the board provides for the elderly are home help services, and bereavement support services.

4. *The Poverty Alleviation Bureau*: This bureau was established to assist in the reduction and elimination of poverty in Barbados.

5. *The Welfare Department*: This department provides a variety of services to families and persons who need assistance in dealing with personal, family and financial problems.

The Ministry of Tourism and International Transport

The Ministry of Tourism and International Transport is the principal public agency charged with the formulation and development of policy, the conduct of research and monitoring of the tourist industry in Barbados. The ministry's role is reflected in its mission statement which reads,

"To provide leadership in the sustainable development of Barbados' tourist industry through the formulation of policy, the provision of timely and quality research, the development and maintenance of industrywide standards and the facilitation of appropriate product development."

The ministry carries out its main functions through a statutory body called "The Barbados Tourism Authority". This authority was established by the Barbados Tourism Act Chapter 342. The functions of this authority are:

1. To promote and facilitate the effective development of Tourism,

2. To encourage the establishment of amenities and facilities necessary for the proper enjoyment of Barbados as a tourist destination;

3. To carry out market research in order to be informed of the needs of the tourist industry; and

4. To register, license and classify tourist accommodation.

The ministry works in conjunction with various agencies to assist it with the development of tourism. These agencies include:

1. The Barbados Hotel and Tourism Association (BHTA) – this agency's primary aim is the promotion, regulation and increase of the tourist industry in Barbados. It is a non-profit organization which was founded in 1956. It is the umbrella body of hotel proprietors. Among the services provided to its members is the computerization of a central hotel reservation service. The association also caters to travel agents in Europe and the United States of America, who are well informed about Barbados and the type of hotel accommodation.

2. The Caribbean Tourism Association (CTA) – This organization was established in January 1989. The CTA's responsibilities are regional and the organization embraces both private and public sector members.

The Tourism Development Corporation (TDC)

This organization was formed in 1987. It is a non-profit organization which comprises members of the private sector in Barbados. Its primary purpose is the development, promotion and marketing of the tourism industry.

The Barbados Tourism Investment Corporation.

This organization is wholly owned by the Barbados Government. Its principal activities include:

1.   The development of properties vested in it by the Government of Barbados;
2.   The promotion and facilitation of tourism investment in Barbados; and
3.   The redevelopment of certain key tourism areas in Barbados, for example, in 2001 the Urban Rehabilitation Unit undertook a project to redevelop and enhance St. Lawrence Gap, a key tourist spot in Barbados.

The Ministry of Commerce, Consumer Affairs and Business Development

In this age of globalization and free trade, Barbados needs to have a well-organized system of business, which is on par with other international regions. To this end, the Ministry of Commerce. Consumer Affairs and Business Development is charged with the administration and development of the business sector in Barbados.

The objectives of this ministry include:
1.   promoting the growth and development of the commercial and business sectors, small businesses, and,
2.   implementing consumer policies and programmes and a national system of business standard.

To achieve these objectives, the ministry carries out its functions through two main agencies. These are the *Fair Trading Commission (FTC) and the Barbados National Standards Institute(BNSI).*

The Fair Trading Commission was established on January 2, 2001 pursuant to the Fair Trading Commission Act Chapter 326 B. It is essentially a regulatory and investigative body, charged with safeguarding the interest of consumers, promoting fair competition and establishing competitive markets in Barbados. For example, if a consumer considers that the quality of a service delivered to him by a particular utility company is substandard, and not in accord with the rate charged on such a service, a complaint may be made to the FTC, which will advise the consumer and investigate the matter.

The ministry is also responsible for the regulation of all consumer and business-related acts including The Utilities Regulation Act Chapter 282 and the Telecommunications Act Chapter 282B.

The Ministry of Industry and International Business

The mission of this ministry is to promote and implement policy that will guarantee the continued economic and social development of Barbados. To this end, the ministry's policies are aimed at the increase in local export, that is, the sale of Barbadian goods produced by local craftsmen and manufacturers. In addition, the ministry is concerned with the establishment of Barbados as a leading business and service centre.

Other governmental ministries include The Ministry of Home Affairs, The Ministry of Agriculture and Rural Development, The Ministry of Labour and Social Security, The Ministry of the Civil Service. The Ministry of Public Works, The Ministry of Housing and Land and the Environment, and The Ministry of Energy and Public Utilities.

Local Government

In addition to the central government which takes care of national problems, many countries have a form of local government which deals with matters which are of a parochial nature. The local government authorities look after matters such as water supply, sewers, public health and sanitation, poor relief, public baths and parks. Barbados once had a system of local government. At first each parish had its own local government called the vestry, which was presided over by an official called a church-warden. Only rate payers in each parish had the franchise. Later, the franchise was extended to all persons 21 years or older as was the case of central government and the island was divided for local government purposes into three areas. Two districts were served by councils; the Northern District Council served the northern parishes like St. Lucy and St. Peter, and the Southern District Council served parishes like St. Philip, St. John and Christ Church. The city of Bridgetown and the parish of St. Michael were served by a city council, which was headed by a mayor.

In 1967, the local government councils were dissolved and the administration of local government affairs was placed into the hands of an Interim Commissioner for Local Government. Eventually, in 1969, some functions of the local government service were transferred to the central government while others, such as the National Assistance Board, the Sanitation and Cemeteries Board, and the Parks and Beaches Commission, now the National Conservation Commission were dealt with by statutory bodies.

From time to time, there is a call for the re-introduction of local government. Those who make this call argue that the matters which are dealt with by local government institutions are not suited for the administration of central government, which should concentrate on national affairs, leaving local affairs in the hands of a more parochial and informal organization.

STATUTORY CORPORATIONS

Besides the civil service, certain statutory bodies have been set up to implement government's policy.

These statutory corporations as they are called are supposed to bring new thinking to bear on public policy. The decision-making process is not expected to be bogged down by 'red-tape' as is the case in the civil service. The legislation setting up these corporations gives them substantial discretion in matters falling within their domain. Sometimes these institutions have not functioned as was expected, primarily because of tight political control and the absence of independence on the part of boards appointed to manage the corporations.

The chairman and members of these statutory bodies are appointed by the minister under whose portfolio they fall. They are not full-time employees, but receive allowances. The day-to-day administration is carried out by a staff appointed by each corporation. Neither the members of these bodies nor their staff is subject to the same regulations as the civil service. The Barbados Labour Party promised in its election manifesto to associate Members of Parliament more closely with the work of these boards, and when it assumed power in 1976, it appointed Members of Parliament as chairmen of some of them. This policy did not continue in subsequent administrations.

Let us take a look at some of these corporations:
1. National Housing Corporation – provides housing for the community. Its principal function is to construct homes for low- and middle-income groups. These houses can either be rented or bought outright where mortgages are arranged for the purchaser.

2. Barbados Investment and Development Corporation – was established by an act of Parliament in 1993. The Barbados Investment

and Development Corporation carries out the functions which were formerly carried out by the Industrial Development Corporation established in 1969 and the Export Promotion Corporation established in 1979. Among the stated functions of the corporation are:

(a) To advise on, promote and facilitate the development of export trade;

(b) To conduct and facilitate research into investment, industrial development and the export of products and services;

(c) To establish, expand and encourage the establishment and expansion of enterprises of goods and services;

(d) To provide financial, technical or other assistance to enterprises engaged in investment, production of goods and services, and exports of goods and services;

(e) To encourage and facilitate investment and the establishment of new enterprises; and

(f) To foster and promote the development of offshore financial services.

In continuing the work of the Industrial Development Corporation, the Barbados Industrial and Development Corporation may acquire property and develop it for industrial use. Its factory buildings are leased to foreign and local entrepreneurs. As a further incentive to encourage the establishment of industries, the Government grants tax-free holidays and remissions of customs duty on plant machinery and raw materials to persons who set up industries which can be classified as pioneer industries. Within the last 25 years, industry in Barbados has expanded, and today, the Barbados Industrial and Development Corporation can boast of more than 10 industrial parks, where a wide range of articles is manufactured for local use and export. The list includes clothing, aluminium ware, handicraft, hockey gloves, bodies for motor buses and electronic equipment. These developments have provided direct employment for several persons.

3. Barbados Tourism Authority is responsible for promoting Barbados as a tourist resort. The board has its headquarters in Barbados, but there are also offices in various parts of the world, including New York, Toronto, London and Caracas. Tourism has now become a major foreign currency earner in Barbados.

Some other statutory corporations are: The Agricultural Development Corporation, The Barbados Marketing Corporation, The Natural Gas Corporation, The Child Care Board, The National Conservation Commission, The Sanitation Services Authority and The Caribbean Broadcasting Corporation.

EXERCISES

1. Is there any advantage to be gained by placing the control of secondary schools into the hands of the boards of management rather than directly under the Ministry of Education?

2. How can parents' participation in education management through governing bodies contribute to national development?

3. Is there a valid case for local government in a country the size of Barbados?

4. Do you consider local government a good training ground for Parliament?

5. Discuss and debate each of the following topics:
    (a) Free secondary education is a luxury which Barbados cannot afford.
    (b) "When a civil servant is appointed to an established post, it is extremely difficult to remove him from the public service."
    (c) Anytime there is a change of government all senior civil servants should be forced to resign their positions."

THINGS TO DO

6. Pay a visit to the Archives Department or the Barbados Museum and write an account of your visit.

7. Explain and discuss the term 'impartial civil service'.

8. Outline the main categories of the civil service. What are their functions?

9. Write short notes on the following:
    (a) Civil service
    (b) Judicial and Legal Services Commission
    (c) Statutory corporations
    (d) Public Service Commission
    (e) Public Service Board of Appeal

10. "Ministers of government have the overall responsibility for the various government departments under their ministries ... the day-to-day planning, supervising and carrying out of policy are in the

hands of a body of permanent workers known as civil servants."
Discuss this statement, giving examples to illustrate your answer.

11. Is the Ministry of Social Transformation a necessary portfolio of
    the Government or another form of wastage of government
    money? Discuss.

12. Why is it necessary for the Ministry of Social Transformation to
    be closely aligned to various agencies?

13. Write short notes on the following agencies which all fall under
    the responsibility of the Ministry of Social Transformation.
    (a)   The National Disabilities Unit
    (b)   The Poverty Eradication Committee
    (c)   The Community Development Department

CHAPTER 7

THE PUBLIC PURSE

"When there is an income tax the just man will pay more and the unjust less on the same amount of income."

Plato (427-347 B. C.) Translation by Benjamin Jowett

Taxation

We often hear our friends and neighbours complaining about the taxes they have to pay, and some persons even ask, "Why do we have to pay taxes, anyway?"

We also hear the same people asking, "Why doesn't the Government do this, why don't they do that?" The only way the Government can do the large number of things it is expected to do is if it collects taxes. Some of the things which our taxes are used for are to provide the water we use, build roads and airports, maintain schools and hospitals, pay the police force and civil servants. What the public is justified in criticizing is the wastage of public funds.

Sometimes the Government receives assistance or borrows money from other governments or financial institutions to assist in financing big projects, but it is not usual for a government to borrow money for the recurrent expenditure of administering the affairs of the country. The largest amount of money it spends to run the country comes from the citizens in the form of taxes. There are two main types of taxation: (a) direct and (b) indirect. When we pay taxes for the property we own, or when we pay income tax, the money comes from us directly and we know exactly how much we have paid. This tax cannot be easily passed on to anyone else, although in the case of property tax, it may influence the rental that is charged for a property. Property tax, income tax and corporation tax are all forms of direct taxation. Did you ever consider that when we buy a postage stamp, the money we pay for it is a form of taxation too?

Customs Duty

Customs duty is a tax imposed upon articles coming into the country. We sometimes hear someone saying that he or she had to pay duty at the airport on articles brought in from overseas, or that duty was charged on gifts sent by relatives or friends abroad. The duty which individuals pay on these goods is only a small amount of the duty received; the greater part comes from businessmen who import things for sale. The importer pays duty on the articles and it is then incorporated into the price and passed on to the consumer. When, therefore, we buy a dress or a shirt, part of the price we pay goes to the revenue as tax.

Normally, the duty charged on basic foodstuff is not very high, otherwise this would prevent poorer people from being able to buy it. On the other hand, the duty charged on luxury goods such as jewellery and clothing, and the duty charged on motor vehicles are usually quite high. It is also usual for duty paid on petrol to be high. When the Government wants to raise additional taxation by means of customs duty, alcoholic drinks and cigarettes are some of the first items on which tax is increased since these are not considered to be essential for human life. Normally, no duty is payable on educational material.

Excise Duty

Excise duty is somewhat similar to customs duty, but instead of its being imposed on imported goods it is imposed on goods manufactured in Barbados. For example, local manufacturers of rum have to pay excise duty on their products.

Value Added Tax

One of the main sources of government revenue, in the form of value added tax, was introduced in Barbados on first January 1997. It is applied to imports and the supply of goods and services. It is a tax on consumption and is included in the final price the consumer pays for goods and services.

With the introduction of value added tax, certain taxes were abolished. These include consumption tax, surcharge on luxury items, service tax, surcharge on rentals, and stamp duty on imports.

The Value Added Tax (VAT) Division of the Customs and Excise Department is the body that is responsible for administering this tax. The Value Added Tax Act, Chapter 87 determines how the tax is imposed in Barbados. There are three rates of tax on goods and services under this system of taxation.

The first is the zero-rated of goods and services. These are goods and services that are taxable but at zero-per cent (0%). These goods include certain prescribed medical devices, certain drugs, crude oil, service charge payable to hotels, guest houses and restaurants, and telecommunication services.

The second is the concessionary rated supplies. This is a 7.5% tax applied to accommodation in inns and guest houses. Not all goods and services are subject to this form of taxation.

The third and most common is the standard-rated goods and services. A standard rate of 15% tax is applied to goods and services sold or provided in Barbados which are not exempt from taxation, zero-rated or concessionary rated. For example, when we purchase certain items from the supermarket or other retail outlet, we often pay VAT on these specific items.

Certain goods and services are exempt from VAT. These exempted supplies include rental of dwelling houses, financial services of banks, medical, dental and paramedical services, educational institutions and water and sewerage service by the Barbados Water Authority, goods and services supplied by a charity, local transportation, e.g., minibus or taxi services.

All businesses charging VAT at on items must be registered with the VAT Division of Customs and Excise Department and display a certificate of VAT registration.

Income Tax

As a rule, people do not like to pay taxes, but it seems as though the tax which is most complained about is income tax. Government takes a part of the salary and wages of all workers who earn above the specified minimum. The taxpayer is granted an allowance for himself, as well as for his wife and children; insurance policies, medical bills and insurance paid on mortgage loans are exempted from income tax. Government can increase or decrease the number of items on which allowances are granted. After these allowances have been deducted, the rest of the worker's earnings is subject to tax in accordance with a formula that has been worked out in advance – the more the taxpayer earns the higher is the level of tax. In fact, it is possible among highly paid persons at some stages for the Government to take as tax, a higher percentage of additional income earned than the tax payer receives for himself.

One complaint that is often made against income tax is that it affects persons who earn a regular weekly wage or monthly salary, while it is very difficult to assess the earnings of self-employed persons, who often get away from paying their share of tax. There are heavy penalties imposed on persons caught making an untrue declaration as to the amount of money they earn.

Under the system known as Pay As You Earn (PAYE), the Government collects its income tax at source, that is, the tax is deducted before the worker receives his pay. It is calculated approximately how much money the worker should earn during the year and each pay day regular deduction is made from his earnings. In this way, the Government has no problem of collecting the tax and the taxpayer is not burdened with having to look for a lump sum at one particular time. At the end of each year, the taxpayer, on a prescribed form, submits his income tax returns which is a statement of all money earned during the year, all the taxes paid and all the allowances for which he is eligible. If he has overpaid his share of taxation, he receives a refund. He has to pay the difference between what should have been, and what was actually paid in case he had underpaid.

On the next page you will see an individual income tax return form.

Besides customs and excise duty income tax and value added tax, there are other forms of taxation. Let us examine some of these taxes and the agencies responsible for collecting them. Some tax collecting agencies in Barbados are:

(1)   The Inland Revenue Department

(2)   The Customs and Excise Department

(3)   Rates and Taxes Division of the Ministry of Finance

(4)   The Treasury Department

(5)   The Registration Department

(6)   The Department of Corporate Affairs and Intellectual Property

(7)   The Land Registration Department

(8)   The Civil Aviation Department

(9)   The General Post Office

INDIVIDUAL INCOME TAX RETURN

FORM A47 - 024

Inland Revenue
Barbados

YEAR OF INCOME

2005

1

FILING DATE ON OR BEFORE APRIL 30, 2006

If there is no label in this space **PRINT** your information below.

Enter your
National Registration Number   and   National Insurance Number

Enter your Occupation / Profession | Sex
☐ Male   ☐ Female

If Married, state your spouse's Last Name, First Name and Initial.

Correct any information shown on the label in the space provided below.

First Name and Initials   ☐ Mr. ☐ Mrs. ☐ Miss

Family or Last Name

Address

Spouse's
National Registration Number   and   National Insurance Number

Tick ✓ the box that applies to your residency in 2005. (Refer to Note 1 Page 4)
☐ Resident   ☐ Non-Resident
If Non-Resident, state the Country of Residence.

Is this your first Return? ☐ Yes   ☐ No   Year

If no, state the income year for which you last filed.
If deceased, state date of death   Year   Month   Day

Tick ✓ the box that applies to your marital status at December 31st, 2005

1 ☐ Single 2 ☐ Married 3 ☐ Separated 4 ☐ Widowed 5 ☐ Divorced

PLEASE COMPLETE ALL RELEVANT INFORMATION ABOVE

For Official use only → **801**

Please turn to Schedule A on page 2 to begin your calculations.   Barbados currency only

Total Assessable Income (Enter from line 290 on page 2)	100	
Total Allowances and Deductions (Enter from line 340 on page 3)	101	
Taxable Income (Subtract line 101 from line 100)	102	
Tax Payable on Taxable Income at line 102 (Refer to Tax Tables)	105	
Amount of Special Taxes (Enter amount from line 463 on page 4)	106	
Total Taxes Payable (Add lines 105 and 106)	110	
Income Tax Deductions (Enter amount from line 200 on page 2)	111	
Total Other Credits (Enter amount from line 360 on page 3)	112	
Total Credits (Add lines 111 and 112)	115	
Net Tax Payable (Subtract line 115 from 110, if line 115 exceeds line 110 enter the excess on line 120 below, otherwise enter on line 116)	116	

Refund Claimed   120

Tax Refund Certificates
(For denominations, complete
Schedule D on Page 4)   121

Refund Cheque ☐   Direct Deposit ☐   122
If Direct Deposit, please state your

Bank / Credit Union Account Number: _____

Name of Bank / Credit Union and Branch: _____

(Attach cheque or money order payable to the Commissioner of Inland Revenue.)
Do not mail cash.
REFER TO NOTE 4 PAGE 4 FOR INFORMATION ON LATE FILING AND LATE PAYMENT PENALTIES.

Less Taxes Prepaid (Refer to note 2 Page 4)   123

Balance Due   124

Amount Due on Filing (Refer to notes 3 & 4 Page 4)   125

Amount Paid on Filing   126

Balance Unpaid   127

Amount Due by Sept. 30th   128

I hereby certify that the information given in this return and in any documents attached is true, correct and complete in every respect and fully discloses my income from all sources.

Signature: _____   Date: _____

Tel. Nos.:
(H) _____

This return was prepared by Self ☐ Yes ☐ No   or by: _____   (W) _____
Tick Box   Please Print Name

IT IS AN OFFENCE TO MAKE A FALSE RETURN   (C) _____

This form is authorised and prescribed by the Commissioner of Inland Revenue

A sample of Individual Tax Return Form

1. The Inland Revenue Department headed by a commissioner of inland revenue is the major collecting agency of direct taxation. The most important taxes which it is responsible for collecting are income tax and corporation tax.

2. The Customs and Excise Department is responsible for the greatest collection of indirect taxation. This department is responsible for the collection of import and excise duties as well as the value added tax. The head of the Customs and Excise Department is the comptroller of customs.

3. The Rates and Taxes Division of the Ministry of Finance is concerned mainly with the collection of property taxes and fees for the licensing of motor vehicles.

4. The Registration Department is chiefly concerned with the registration of births, deaths and marriages. It collects fees for issuing various types of certificates including certificates of birth, death and marriage. It is also responsible for collecting registration fees from professional persons. The head of the Registration Department is the Registrar, whose duties include the service of Registrar of the Supreme Court.

5. The Department of Corporate Affairs and Intellectual Property is responsible for the registration of companies, business, trade marks and patents. It is headed by a registrar of corporate affairs.

6. The Land Registration Department which is headed by the registrar of lands collects taxes on the transfer of land as well as fees for the registration of land transfers.

7. The Civil Aviation Department collects fees from aircraft landing in Barbados. There is also a government departure tax which is

paid by all passengers leaving the country. This is collected by the airline agents and paid to the Civil Aviation Department.

8.   The General Post Office is responsible for the collection of all stamp duties. Besides postage stamps, this department sells stamps to be placed on documents, for example, insurance policies, documents for the sale of land, and receipts for sums in excess of $10. The head of the post office is the Postmaster-General.

All the taxes collected along with other government revenue go into a central fund known as the Consolidated Fund. No money can be withdrawn from this fund without the permission of Parliament.

The Budget

Since most people need more things than their money can buy, they often have to decide what should be given priority. To assist them in planning, some persons make a list of how their money is to be spent – how much must be spent on food, clothing, shelter, entertainment and other needs. This is called budgeting. Making a budget and living within it is considered good housekeeping.

Each year the Government, like a good housekeeper, has to consider how much money is required to manage the country, how this money is to be raised and how it will be allocated to satisfy the competing claims on government revenue. Government's business is too complex for it to budget on a weekly or monthly basis; it budgets for a year. The Government's financial year is not the same as the calendar year; it runs from 1st April to 31st March.

Besides showing us figures of receipts and expenditure, the budget gives us some insight into the policy of the Government. In deciding to raise money, the Government has a variety of means it can use, and the choice that is actually made is determined by the philosophy of the particular government. For example, government may believe that parents with children of school age should have more money to assist with their education; this belief can be reflected in the granting of additional allowances to such persons. There may be great need for additional revenue but instead of establishing a national lottery, government might place additional taxation on cigarettes and alcoholic drinks; this could be a direct result of its anti-gambling policy. Taxing cigarettes and alcoholic beverages could also be a means to recover health expenditure caused by alcoholic beverage and cigarette consumption.

Another factor which government has to consider is the long-term effect which its taxation policy will have on the economy. Burdensome rates of income tax could cause workers to lose all interest in producing beyond a certain level. Too large a tax burden within the hotel business can cause a reduction in the number of visitors to the country and this, in turn, can result in many workers in the tourist industry becoming unemployed. You see, therefore, that the Government has to he very careful when it is preparing the budget and fiscal policy.

The preparation of the national budget is a very confidential affair, because if some persons knew on what articles taxes were being increased they would, in order to avoid the additional taxation and to make a profit, buy these items in large quantity before the new tax was imposed.

To enable the Minister of Finance and his advisers to plan the Estimates of Expenditure, all government departments submit estimates of their requirements for the ensuing year; it is then left to the Minister of Finance to try to satisfy the requirements of the various departments within the limits of the budget.

After the minister has decided how the money is to be raised, he has to obtain the approval of Parliament to raise it, for no new tax can be imposed without parliamentary approval. Similarly, before any of the revenue is spent, Parliament has to approve the expenditure; this is done in the annual Appropriation Act.

In March of every year, the Minister of Finance presents the Estimates of Revenue and Expenditure to Parliament. The Estimates of

Expenditure are made up of (a) statutory and (b) other expenditure. Statutory expenditure is governed by law and is not debated in Parliament. This type of expenditure is charged on the Consolidated Fund by provisions of the Constitution or other law. It includes the salaries of the Governor-General, the judiciary, the Auditor-General, and the Director of Public Prosecutions. The Appropriation Bill, made up of the amount of other expenditure allocated to all ministries and departments, is debated in Parliament. This must be completed on or before 31st March every year.

During the debate on the estimates, Members of Parliament take the opportunity to comment on the work of the various departments as well as the general policy of the Government. While the Government members usually support the proposals, the Opposition normally takes the opportunity to criticize the Government's policy and show how they would have managed the country more efficiently had they been in power.

It was customary for the Minister of Finance to go to the House of Assembly later in the year to outline to the members of the House the details of the budget and the Government's fiscal policy for the ensuing year. This was known as the Budget Speech. The present Prime Minister, Owen Arthur, has changed that practice and now presents his budgetary proposals shortly before he presents the Estimates of Revenue and Expenditure.

The control of the revenue by Parliament is one of the outstanding features of a democracy, for it gives the citizens through their elected representatives the opportunity to examine, criticize, and even change what has been proposed.

In order to ensure that the money voted by Parliament is used for the purpose for which it was intended, the Auditor-General presents an annual report to a committee of Parliament known as the Public Accounts Committee. By tradition, this committee is headed by the Leader of the Opposition.

EXERCISES

1. What are the main sources of government revenue in Barbados?

2. What is the purpose of supplementary estimates?

3. Why do you think we pay taxes on property?

4. What is the difference between customs and excise duty?

5. What is the difference between capital and recurrent expenditure?

6. Why is money not allowed to be taken from the Consolidated Fund without the approval of Parliament?

7. Explain each of the following:
    (a) Estate and succession duty
    (b) Corporation tax
    (c) The functions of the Auditor-General

8. "Income tax is an unfair form of taxation and should be abolished." Discuss.

9. "Value added tax is a necessary addition to the public purse in Barbados." Discuss.

THINGS TO DO

10. With the assistance of your teacher complete an income tax return form.

Houses at Lower Barney, St. Michael, built by government for persons whom we relocated from Church Village, Bridgetown to provide additional land area for the use of the Central Bank of Barbados.

Prime Minister Right Honourable Owen Arthur being sworn in as Prime Minister of Barbados after General Elections of 23 May, 2003, in the presence of Governor-General, Sir Clifford Husbands and Mrs. Patricia Layne, private secretary to the Governor-General.

Barbados Community College - A tertiary institution providing training in academic, technical and professional subjects leading to the award of associate degrees. This institution will form part of the proposed University College of Barbados.

Pupils of Bay Primary School, Bayville, St. Michael, one of government's primary schools.

Arawak Cement Plant, located at Checker Hall, St. Lucy. This plant was established in April 1984 as a joint venture between the governments of Barbados and Trinidad & Tobago.

Central Bank of Barbados located at Tom Adams Finanical Centre, Spry Street, Bridgetown.

Government House, St. Michael, Barbados, the official residence of the Governor-General of Barbados.

Hilton Hotel - One of Barbados' leading hotels situated on the south coast of the island. It provides accommodation and conference facilities for the use by visitors and locals.

Parliament Buildings, Bridgetown, where the House of Assembly and Senate meet.

Supreme Court Building where the High Court and Court of Appeal of Barbados hear trails.

Treasury Building in which is located the office of the Commissioner of Inland Revenue.

United Nations Building — The offices of the United Nations agencies in Barbados (other than WHO and PAHO) are accommodated in this building.

Broad Street, Bridgetown — Barbados' main shopping area.

A crowd assembled in the Public Buildings Yard outside Parliment to cheer parliamentarians as they enter for the Prime Minister's presentation of the Annual Financial Statement — 2006.

Frank Walcott Building, Culloden Road, St. Michael, which houses the National Insurance Office. The building is named for National Hero, the Right Excellent Sir Frank Walcott, former trade unionist.

Prime Minister, Right Honourable Arthur Owen arriving in Parliament to present the Annual Financial Statement — 2006.

The Cave Hill campus of the University of the West Indies.

CHAPTER 8
IMPORTANT INSTITUTIONS

"Everyone has the right to freedom of thought, conscience and religion; this includes freedom to change his religion or belief ... "

Article 19, Universal Declaration of Human Rights

The Church

The Church is a very important institution in the life of most Barbadians. For many years the Church has played a leading role in the education of the citizens, especially in the provision of schools. Today, the Government has taken over the responsibility for the majority of the schools, but the great influence of the Church remains. Some churches are even accused of influencing the outcome of national elections according to the position taken by their leaders. The clergy's justification for dealing with political matters is that they are concerned not only with the souls of their congregation, but also with their material well-being. Whether we agree with the Church's participation in active politics or not, our democratic way of life affords it that right.

Within two years of its settlement, Barbados was served by the clergy of the Anglican Church and from the outset there was a very close relationship between State and Church. Up to 1969, the Anglican Church was the established Church and the members of its clergy were paid by the State. In 1969, the Anglican Church was disestablished and the Government ceased to be responsible for the salary of the clergy. From that time there has been no State Church. Barbadians have complete freedom of worship guaranteed by the Constitution, and everyone may worship as he or she pleases. There are over 100 denominations in the country today, with Anglican being the predominant denomination. Other denominations include the Methodists and Moravians who first established missions in the 18th century, Baptists, Jehovah's Witnesses, Seventh Day Adventists, Christian Scientists, Pilgrim Holiness and several Pentecostal groups. There are also small groups of Jews, Hindus and Muslims.

No special permission is required to start a church, but if ministers wish to perform marriages, they have to apply to the Ministry of Legal Affairs to be appointed as marriage officers.

The fact that all these religions and denominations can exist side by side is testimony of our democratic way of life. The good citizen learns to respect the beliefs of others, and even if he does not agree with another person's way of worship, he is tolerant and agrees with the person's right to worship as he thinks fit.

Political Parties

J.S. Coleman in his book, *Political Parties and National Integration in Tropical Africa*, described political parties as "associations formally organized with the explicit and declared purpose of acquiring and for maintaining legal control either singly or in coalition or electoral competition with some similar associations over the personnel and the policy of the Government of an actual or prospective sovereign state".

The chief function of a political party, therefore, is to secure the election of its members to Parliament, with a view to carrying out a particular policy. It informs the electorate of its philosophy and normally publishes a document known as a manifesto, in which it sets out what programmes it would pursue, if elected to form the Government and the means it would adopt to carry out these programmes.

Some states permit the legal existence of only one political party. This system is known as the one-party system. Barbados has adopted the multi-party system, which permits the legal existence of any number of parties, but normally there are only two prominent parties which contest elections. Full democracy cannot be practised where only one group monopolizes the political affairs of a country.

In order to keep in touch with the rank and file members of the party, branches known as constituency branches are usually established in each electoral division. The constituency branches through their representatives on the central committee, keep the executive abreast of the happenings in the constituency and keep the constituency members up to date, with the plans and programmes of the party. It is these branches too, which must normally approve of parliamentary candidates for their constituency and sometimes submit the candidates to the central executive, to be considered as candidates for election to Parliament.

In order to arouse public interest in everyday affairs and to encourage the electorate to vote for its members at election time, political parties often organize programmes of political education and issue statements on public issues. This activity is accelerated when an election is imminent. The various parties make use of newspapers, radio and television to publicize their candidates and programmes. One common means of addressing the public is the mass meeting where hundreds gather to hear the case put forward for the various parties. In spite of the increased use of the mass media, the public meeting is still very popular in Barbados. Although some persons believe that it is seen more as a means of entertainment than education, the public meetings have retains their popularity.

The first political party in Barbados was born as a result of the 1937 civil disturbances in Barbados. It was obvious that the supremacy of the white aristocracy was being challenged by the growing educated black middle class which, along with some of the black masses, had shown that they were no longer satisfied socially, politically and economically. It was only a matter of time before a leader would emerge to champion the cause of the labouring classes. It is true that there were organizations such as the Liberal Party headed by Samuel Jackman Prescod during the 1840s and the Democratic League founded by Charles Duncan O'Neal in 1924, but their organization and structure were not like that of the political party as we know it today.

In March 1938, Hope Stevens, a native of Tortola, but then residing in New York, met in Barbados with a group of Barbadians and saw the birth of the Barbados Labour Party. Among the stated objectives of the organization was the desire:

"To provide political expression for all the law-abiding inhabitants of this island, enabling them to participate in the development of democratic institutions, promote the social and economic improvement of its people and assist in the extension of all principles of good government."

The 1940 General Elections saw, for the first time in the history of the country, an election in which a political party, with a clearly defined programme, offered a slate of candidates to be elected to the House of Assembly.

In the 1944 elections, the Congress Party, led by W.A. Crawford, entered candidates for the General Election and performed creditably. Two years later, it entered into a coalition with the Barbados Labour Party to ensure that the working class movement had a clear majority in Parliament. Other parties which have existed in Barbados include the Electors Association, which represented the mercantile interest. Its name was later changed to the Progressive Conservative Party, and later to the Barbados National Party. The People's Progressive Movement has never been successful in any national elections. In the 1970s, another party, the People's Democratic Party, was launched, but this too has never been represented in Parliament. The Worker's Party of Barbados, a left-wing party, contested unsuccessfully one seat in the general election of 1986. In 1988, four members of the Democratic Labour Party resigned from the party and formed the National Democratic Party. In the General Elections of 1991, one of the candidates of the National Democratic

Party gained a seat in the House of Assembly. The Barbados Labour Party dominated the political life of Barbados until 1961 when it lost power to the Democratic Labour Party, a group which had broken away from it in 1955. The development of political parties in the country was among the factors which influenced social and economic development of the country.

Trade Unions

"Everyone has the right to form and to join trade unions for the protection of his interests."

Article 23 (4) Universal Declaration of Human Rights

The Trade Union Act of Barbados describes a trade union as any combination whether temporary or permanent, the principal purposes of which are, under its constitution, the regulation of the relations between workmen and employers, or between workmen and workmen or between employers and employers.

Trade unions appear in the news often when there is a strike, that is, when the members of the union, in furtherance of an industrial dispute, withdraw their services from their employers. The strike action is probably the most effective weapon of the trade union, but usually this action is taken only as a last resort.

Long before strike action is taken, the union would have been in discussion with the employers in an effort to decide on such matters as pay, fringe benefits and working conditions of its members. Normally, it is only after negotiations have broken down that strike action is taken. Sometimes, however, workers go on strike without the sanction of their union; these strikes are known as 'wildcat strikes'. Workers employed in certain essential services such as the electricity company, water works, police and fire services, are prohibited by law from striking.

The right to join a trade union is one of the fundamental rights of every Barbadian citizen. Article 20 (1) of the United Nations Universal Declaration of Human Rights which Barbados supports states:

"Everyone has the right to peaceful assembly and association with others."

Article 23 (4) states:
"Everyone has the right to form and join trade unions for the protection of his interests."

When Barbados became independent, it enshrined into the Constitution the guarantee of freedom of every citizen to belong to trade unions or other associations for the protection of his interests. Today, we take this right for granted, but we should remember that it did not always exist.

The Trade Union Act was passed in 1939 and came into force on 1st August 1940. It was only on the passing of this act that trade union activity, including the right to strike, could be legally carried on. Later, the strike weapon became more effective when, in 1964, legislation was passed permitting peaceful picketing, that is, it became lawful for trade unions in furtherance of a dispute "to attend at or near a place where a person resides or carries on business, for the purpose of personally communicating or obtaining information or of peacefully persuading anyone to work or not to work".

In 1939, when the Trade Union Act was introduced, it was sought to include the right to peaceful picketing, but the clause was rejected by the Legislative Council where a majority of members felt it could be a cause of disturbance. Picketing is a useful means by which the trade union can attract sympathizers to its cause where there is a dispute.

The Barbados Workers Union (BWU)

The first union to register under the act was the Barbados Workers' Union, the industrial arm of the Barbados Progressive League as the Barbados Labour Party was then called. This union is a general workers union and was registered on 4th October 1941. Today, it is the biggest trade union in Barbados and has a membership of over 25,000 persons. This union is organized into divisions which represent various categories of workers in several fields of employment, including construction, manufacturing and industry, banking, agriculture, government and statutory boards.

The objectives of the union include securing the complete organization of all workers in trade unions, obtaining and maintaining just wages, reasonable working hours and generally protecting the interest of its members.

The union is governed by an Executive Council, which is elected at an annual delegates' conference, which is held in the month of August. The day-to-day administration is carried on by the union's staff headed by the general-secretary who is a member of the executive council. The general-secretary is the chief executive officer of the union. He is elected by a ballot at the annual conference and holds office at the pleasure of the union.

The union has been a vital source of social and economic change for this country. Its many achievements include advocating for passing of legislation to provide benefits for the workers. These include maternity leave, unemployment benefits, national insurance and social security, and severance payment. Barbadian workers have thus been able to secure an improved standard of living and work conditions.

Since the formation of the first trade union, there have been other unions of employees. Two other unions registered at present are:

(1)   The National Union of Public Workers, which represents the majority of civil servants.

(2)   The Barbados Union of Teachers, which represents many members of the teaching profession.

The Congress of Trade Unions and Staff Associations of Barbados (CTUSAB)

The Congress of Trade Unions and Staff Associations of Barbados (CTUSAB) is an umbrella body for organized labour, and plays a key role in mobilizing and uniting action by various union members, on matters such as productivity, incomes and competitiveness in the country in relation to the Barbadian worker.

CTUSAB is the umbrella body for trade unions including Barbados Workers Union, National Union of Public Workers, Barbados Union of Teachers, Barbados Registered Nurses Association and Barbados Secondary Teachers Union. Its membership also includes the staff associations of the fire service, police and prisons.

The modern trade union now has a wide range of activities. Its chief function is still to bargain collectively for employees and ensure that they receive just wages and conditions of service and to support the members if the union considers that they are being treated unjustly. In addition, the trade union is engaged in the education of its members, making them aware not only of trade unionism, but of other aspects of life in the society in which they live. It also encourages its members to save by the establishment of credit unions.

The Labour College is the educational arm of the Barbados Workers' Union and provides courses for trade unionists from Barbados and other countries of the Caribbean. Other activities of the union include the provision of housing for its members, the payment of allowances during a strike, and assistance with funeral expenses.

Since the trade union represents a large proportion of the population, its leaders are often invited to be members of government committees to represent the interest of workers.

It is sometimes debated whether a trade union should be actively engaged in party politics. Since there are valid arguments on both sides, the final decision on this matter should be left to the members of each union. One may note, however, that trade unionism and politics are so closely related that often the trade union movement acts as a training ground for politicians.

The organization of most unions is designed to ensure some measure of participation of the rank and file in the decision-making process. The supreme ruling body of a trade union is its annual delegates' conference which is composed of representatives from its various divisions or organizations. This delegates' conference elects an executive which is responsible for the union's policy between conferences.

ORGANIZATION OF THE BARBADOS WORKERS' UNION

ANNUAL DELEGATES' CONFERENCE – held in the month of August

EXECUTIVE COUNCIL – Elected at annual conference; responsible for the government and conduct of its business.

Officers of the Council
>President
>Vice-President
>Treasurer
>General-secretary
>Members
>Trustees

ADMINISTRATION – DAY-TO-DAY

Departments
>Education
>Industrial relations
>Finance and administration
>Public relations and communications
>Counselling and wellness

We tend to think that trade unions are organizations of employees only, but as the act provides, there are also employers' unions. These are formed to protect the interest of employers and to represent them in disputes with the employees' unions. Among the registered employers' unions in Barbados is the Barbados Employers' Confederation.

Barbados Employers' Confederation

The Barbados Employers' Confederation, which was formed in 1956, is a registered trade union of employers. Its membership comprises individual employers and associations of employers. The principal function of the confederation is to regulate the relations between employers and employees and to promote the interest of employers in the country. It acts as the representative body of employers and advises its members on existing laws, proposed legislation or other industrial matters which could affect them. The confederation also represents employers at disputes, industrial negotiations, conciliation or enquiries. Another function of the confeder-ation is to assist its members in upgrading the skills of their employ-ees by conducting training courses for them.

The Press

'Here shall the press the people right, maintain, unaw'd by influence and unbrib'd by gain; ...''

Joseph Story (1779-1845)

The communications media have a very important role to play in a democratic country. Indeed, it is one of the bulwarks of democracy, for not only does it provide us with news, but it serves as a forum for the expression of opinions. The press is a very influential instrument in shaping public opinion. Every day, thousands of newspapers are sold, thus the words of a few writers, when they are read by so many persons, can influence the opinion of a great section of the community.

The widespread use of radio and television has caused the influence of the communications media to be even greater, for they allow the speaker the opportunity to use his voice effectively in trying to persuade his listeners. In the case of television, the use of gestures and appropriate facial expression act further to increase the effect the speaker can have on his audience.

Advertisers are fully aware of the dependence people have on the news media and exploit this dependence to their advantage. So great is the confidence some have in the news media that often a person's only justification for a particular point of view is: "I read it in the newspaper."

As was mentioned earlier, one of the characteristics of a democracy is freedom of the press. This freedom does not mean freedom to libel others, nor should it be interpreted as freedom to use the press dishonestly, to further the ends of particular sections of the community. Rather it should be regarded as freedom to keep the community honestly informed. Journalists have the very important duty to the community to keep it honestly informed. They should not suppress news because it does not support their own point of view; neither should they report untruths or half-truths. They should at all times be impartial.

Some politicians, as well as representatives of economic and other interests, try to control what news the public is allowed to receive, so as to ensure that only reports favourable to them are presented. This is done in several ways: one means is to take control of ownership of the media and then prevent dissemination of any news that is not acceptable to them. In some countries, the Government makes it difficult for opposition groups to publish newspapers. The difficulty may be created for publishers to obtain a licence to import newsprint. Those publishers who seem not to support government's views often experience great difficulty in obtaining the import licence. Another method is for government to demand large sums to be deposited as a bond before permission to publish a newspaper is granted. The large sum of money is often impossible to be obtained by publishers and they are, therefore, unable to operate their business. Similar difficulties can be experienced by operators of the electronic media.

In a democracy, the citizens must not take freedom of the press for granted and think that it will always remain so. They should be very vigilant and protest against any attempt that is being made to muzzle freedom of expression no matter from which quarter it comes. Dictators are so aware of the power of the press that among their first acts is that of gaining control of the press. Attempts to control the press do not come only from politicians; economic pressures are also brought to bear on the media to ensure that its views are sympathetic to the philosophy and policy of the interests exerting the pressure.

The alert citizen, therefore, has to be careful about not being misled by what he reads in the newspaper or what he hears on radio and television. Instead of assuming that whatever is presented must be correct, the citizen has to weigh all sides of an argument carefully and then arrive at his own conclusion. No persuasive or emotional presentation of one point of view should be allowed to prevent the alert citizen from arriving at his own independent judgement.

We should always remember that a free press is a very necessary requirement for the existence of a true democracy.

Barbados Chamber of Commerce

Under the mixed-economy system, much of the prosperity of a country depends upon the commercial activity of the private sector. It is important that there be cooperation between the Government and the private sector to ensure not only that maximum wealth is produced, but that it is used for the benefit of the entire community. To co-ordinate its activities and protect its interests there are various organizations formed among the private sector; the largest of these is the Barbados Chamber of Commerce and Industry.

In 1825, an organization called Commercial Hall was formed. This organization was incorporated by an Act of Parliament in 1868. The name was changed in 1909 to The Barbados Chamber of Commerce. In 1983, the act was repealed and a new act enacted, through which the name was further changed to The Barbados Chamber of Commerce and Industry.

Among its stated objectives are the promotion and encouragement of the development of manufacturing operations of goods to proper standards and grades, assistance in securing markets for new material and finished products and the encouragement of customers to use locally produced products. Some of its activities are done through co-operation with other organizations such as the Barbados Manufacturers' Association and the Barbados Employers' Confederation.

Government recognizes the Chamber of Commerce as the representative of the private sector. Matters, therefore, which are likely to affect the body, are normally referred to the chamber for comments. The chamber is represented on many boards and committees, both private and public.

The Central Bank of Barbados

"Money is to an economy as oil is to an engine".

There are many banks in Barbados where members of the public may deposit money, draw cheques, obtain loans and receive a host of other services. These banks are known as commercial banks.

The Central Bank of Barbados is a special bank which serves a different purpose from the commercial banks. It was established in April 1972 by an Act of Parliament to:

(a) Regulate the issue, supply, availability and international exchange of money;

(b) Promote a monetary stability;

(c) Promote a sound financial structure;

(d) Foster the development of money and capital markets in Barbados;

(e) Foster credit and exchange conditions conducive to the orderly and sustained economic development of Barbados.

The Central Bank has many functions besides the traditional issuing of currency and the withdrawing and destroying of old currency notes.

The bank manages the foreign exchange reserves of the country and advises the Government on monetary matters. It also supervises the operations of the commercial banks, to ensure that credit is made available to the productive sectors of the economy, so that activities like industry and agriculture may be developed.

The bank monitors the rate of interest commercial banks pay on deposits and charge on loans and controls the margins they charge on foreign currencies. If too much money is spent on commodities such as expensive motor cars, we would find that the country would not have enough foreign exchange to pay for them. Moreover, the foreign exchange spent on luxury goods could be better utilized in the purchase of imported equipment and raw materials for building the industrial base. The Central Bank, therefore, controls commercial bank credit by placing limits on the total amount they lend for the purchase of consumer durables and luxury goods, in order to prevent a depletion of the country's foreign exchange reserves. The Central Bank operates also as a bankers' bank and a lender of last resort. In this respect, it makes loans to commercial banks in times of tight liquidity; that is, when ready cash is not freely available.

To carry out its business, the bank is divided into various departments. Besides the secretariat which is responsible for general administration, the departments are:

(a) Banking and currency,

(b) Bank supervision,

(c) Exchange control,

(d) Research, and

(e) Export credit insurance.

The banking department acts as a clearing house for the commercial banks. Each working day, representatives of the commercial banks meet at the Central Bank to adjust their accounts according to the number of cheques drawn on them.

Government keeps control of foreign exchange transactions. If one wants to send foreign exchange from the country, approval must be had from the Central Bank. It is the Exchange Control Department that is responsible for this aspect of the bank's work.

In order for the various departments to carry out their functions effectively, it is necessary for them to have accurate up-to-date information. This service is provided by the research department which collects, compiles and analyses statistical data for the use of the Central Bank. It also produces publications not only for the Central Bank, but for government officials and other interested parties.

During 1977, the Central Bank formally established its export credit insurance and guarantee department in support of government's efforts to expand exports. This department provides credit insurance to local exporters.

The Central Bank in cooperation with the Barbados Chamber of Commerce also runs a securities exchange. This forms the nucleus of a money and capital market where more efficient trading in shares and debentures can take place.

The important thing about the Central Bank of Barbados is that it is the institution through which the Government exercises discretion in monetary management.

Voluntary Organizations

'A community is like a ship; every man ought to he prepared to take the helm"

Henrith Ibsen (1828-1 906)

Voluntary organizations comprise groups of persons who come together of their volition to attain a common goal, without expectation of financial reward for their effort. Such organizations can perform a pivotal function in improving the quality of life in our community. Examples of these organizations in Barbados are the Lions Club, Toastmasters, National Association of Alcoholics Barbados (NASAB), Girl Guides, Boy Scouts, Young Men's Christian Association, Young Women's Christian Association, parent education agencies such as PAREDOS, the Consumers' League, and the several affiliated church organizations. Let us examine the role of one of the above-mentioned organizations.

The NASAB consists of a group of persons who recognize the personal and social ills which are caused by alcoholic beverages. They set about to help sick persons who are addicted to alcohol or persons who, though not suffering from alcoholic addiction, desire help in severing links with alcoholic beverages. At another level, NASAB conducts clinics for youngsters to educate them about the dangers posed by alcoholic beverages. Their activities require several man hours of varying levels of skills. They raise their finances from fund-raising activities, which may take the form of covenants, tea parties or raffles. Most other voluntary organizations are structured along lines similar to NASAB's.

Voluntary organizations provide an avenue for developing skills in leadership and fellowship. They constitute the meeting point for persons of all classes to come together in the attainment of a common goal. To the extent that they function well they strengthen the bonds in a society. They also provide the more fortunate members of our society with the opportunity to make a contribution towards the uplifting of their less fortunate fellow men.

Organized voluntary effort can be regarded as a necessary condition to ensure the proper functioning of the democratic system. Where voluntary organizations flourish, public sector resources can achieve more, because they will be complemented by private sector resources. In addition, the citizens will be more motivated to take care of public property thereby avoiding the unnecessary spending of public funds on replacements instead of creating additional facilities for public use. A society in which voluntary organizations are vibrant will act as an effective check on its leaders. We are aware of the familiar saying "power corrupts". Hence the necessity for all citizens to be vigilant in guarding their rights. Perhaps the most effective method we can employ to safeguard our rights is active involvement in the shaping of our society. A good preparation for the future involvement of young people in the work of voluntary organizations is participation in the activities of the Boy Scout and Girl Guide movements and other youth organizations.

EXERCISES

1. Discuss and debate each of the following topics.
   (a) "All newspapers should be controlled by the Government."
   (b) "Strikes disrupt the country and should be forbidden."
   (c) "Barbados has enough religious denominations and no new ones should be allowed to be formed."
   (d) "The free-enterprise system is responsible for the majority of the ills of the country."

2. What do the following mean?
   (a) Collective agreement
   (b) Arbitration
   (c) Picketing
   (d) Lock-out
   (e) Sick-out
   (f) Go-slow
   (g) Essential services
   (h) Industrial action

3. What were some of the benefits obtained by employees as a result of the following acts?
   (a) The Holiday with Pay Act
   (b) The Factories Act
   (c) The Severance Payment Act

4. If government nationalized all the commercial banks would we still need a central bank? Discuss.

5. The Chamber of Commerce is sometimes sarcastically referred to as an unofficial arm of government. Discuss.

6. List three voluntary organizations in Barbados and give an account of the work each performs.

7. Show how participation in the work of voluntary organizations can help to strengthen democracy.

8. Discuss and debate each of the following topics.
   (a) "Voluntary workers are the life blood of a democracy."
   (b) "All young people should be required to perform national service for at least one year."

9. (a) Do you think that the clergy should be involved in politics? State reasons for and against this involvement.
   (b) How can voluntary organizations assist government in providing goods and services for its citizens? Support your answer by giving examples of the work of three such voluntary organizations.

10. "Freedom of the press is a myth." Discuss.

THINGS TO DO

1. Find out the names of as many registered trade unions in Barbados as you can. Make a list of them.

2. Compile a list of the newspapers published in Barbados. Include the following information: -
   (a) Frequency of publication
   (b) Name of the editor
   (c) State the different points of view represented by the different papers.

3. Ask students who belong to voluntary organizations to explain why they joined and to give an account of the activities of the organization to the class.

CHAPTER 9

SYMBOLS OF INDEPENDENCE

"A thoughtful mind when it sees a nation's flag sees not the flag only, but the nation itself."

Henry Ward Beecher (1813-1887)

If we attend an international function or visit the United Nations when the General Assembly is in session, we will see displayed the flags of the member countries. One thing that becomes evident is that no two countries have the same flag.

Like other independent nations, Barbados has its own flag. It also has a coat of arms, a national anthem, national pledge, national motto and national flower. These are all national symbols or emblems. The National Emblems and National Anthem of Barbados (Regulations) Act Chapter 300A regulates the use of these national emblems. These emblems must be treated with the greatest of care and it is an offence to mutilate, cut, tear or in any way deface any of these national emblems. In addition, they may not be used in connection with a business, trade or other activity without a licence from the Government of Barbados. These national emblems are the property of the Barbados Government; therefore, the copyright in the words and music of the national anthem and the design of the national emblems is vested in the Crown, not the original authors.

The Flag

The first flags which were used thousands of years ago were not made of cloth; they were made of the skin of animals or the feathers of birds. Hunters and warriors used them so that everyone would know who they were.

From early times, armies, when they were going to battle, took their standards to serve as a rallying point for their soldiers. The loss of the standard was considered a great disgrace, while it would be held aloft with pride at the time of victory. Today, the flag of a nation still remains a symbol of pride.

Some years ago when Barbados was still a British colony, school children would face the Union Jack daily and salute it as a mark of respect. Today, we are not called upon to salute our flag except on some ceremonial occasions. But, nevertheless, the same degree of respect or even more should be shown for our national flag; it should never be considered a mere piece of cloth attached to a stick, but rather as one of the symbols of independence of which we are proud.

When the flag is flown, certain rules ought to be observed.

1. The flag should not be allowed to become tattered.
2. The flag-mast upon which it is flown must be painted white.
3. The flag should not remain on the flagpole after sunset.
4. The flag should not be flown upside down, or with the trident inverted except as a signal of distress.
5. No flag is to be flown to the right of or above the national flag except at foreign embassies or consulates.
6. The flag is flown at half-staff during periods of national mourning.

If we were to visit a Barbadian Embassy abroad, we would see the flag flying before the house or office of the ambassador; this shows the entire world where our representative may be found and this office is treated as Barbadian soil. The nation's flag is also flown on merchant ships registered in Barbados. At state funerals, it is used to drape the coffin of the deceased.

Before independence in 1966, a competition was organized for the selection of a design for a national flag. From over 1000 entries the present flag, designed by Mr. Grantley W. Prescod, an art teacher, was selected. The flag comprises three equal vertical bars. The outer two bars are of ultramarine signifying the sea, the centre bar is of gold signifying the sun and sand of its beaches, and there is a broken trident in the centre. The trident which appears on the flag of colonial Barbados is that of the mythical sea god, Neptune. The trident is broken to suggest our break from our colonial past.

The National Anthem

At the Olympic Games and other international sporting events, when an athlete wins a gold medal he stands proud, as he hears his national anthem being played. In Barbados the national anthem is played at the beginning or end of a public performance, when the Queen, a member of the royal family, or Governor-General appears at a public function and on ceremonial and official occasions.

Just as we need always to show respect for the flag, we must also be respectful to our national anthem. One way of doing so is by standing at attention when the anthem is being played. As a further sign of respect, all men with covered heads should remove the covering. In some countries, persons who do not stand during the playing of their national anthem are punished; this is not the case in Barbados. We should not have to be forced to respect our symbols; we should respect them out of pride for our independence.

One verse of our national anthem is usually played, consisting of the first 12 bars of the verse and the last four of the chorus. The anthem should not be distorted, satirized or parodied in poetry or song; neither should it be played in any other tempo than that officially recognized by the Government of Barbados. On official occasions when more than one anthem is to be played, the national anthem of Barbados must be played last.

Two Barbadians were responsible for producing our national anthem. The music was composed by Mr. C. Van Roland Edwards.

In 1967, it was re-arranged by Inspector Prince Cave of The Royal Barbados Police Band. The words were written by Mr. Irvin Burgie.

The Coat of Arms

The Barbados Coat of Arms was presented by Her Majesty Queen Elizabeth II on the 14th February, 1966, on a visit to Barbados.

The Coat of Arms of Barbados is the official seal of the Government of Barbados and may not be used or reproduced without the approval of the Government of Barbados. On the shield of the coat of arms, there is a bearded fig tree from which it is alleged that Barbados derived its name. Two Pride of Barbados flowers are found at the apex of the shield. The crest displays the raised fore-arms of a Barbadian holding two crossed sugar canes above the helmet and a mantling. Supporting the shield on one side is a pelican; this is reminiscent of Pelican, the little island which was merged with the mainland at the time of the construction of the Deep Water Harbour. On the other side is a dolphin, symbolic of the fishing industry. Our nation's motto 'Pride and Industry' appears beneath the shield. The coat of arms was designed by Mr. Neville Clarke Connell who was a student of Heraldry.

The Motto

Our motto **'Pride and Industry'**, is supposed to describe the reputation of island's inhabitants. We should, therefore, all strive to live up to this reputation in everything we do.

The National Pledge

The national pledge was written by Mr. Lester Vaughan, a former teacher and education officer of primary schools. Mr. Vaughn was born in 1910 at Simon's Saint Andrew.

The choice of the national pledge was announced on the 2nd April 1973 by the Hon. Erskine Sandiford, then Minister of

Education, Youth Affairs, Community Development and Sport. Mr. Vaughan's composition was selected from 167 entries, in a Government-sponsored competition for the composition of the national pledge.

In an effort to teach our children to appreciate and to be loyal to their country at an early age, the national pledge is recited in most government and private schools. It would be a good thing if adults also learn it and live up to the sentiments it expresses.

The National Flower

The National Flower of Barbados is the Pride of Barbados, commonly known as the Dwarf Poinciana or Flower Fence. Sighting of this flower was first recorded in 1657. It blooms year round in several varieties. It is fiery red in appearance with yellow margin on each of its five petals in a pyramidal inflorescence. The national flower appears on the nation's coat of arms.

EXERCISES

1. Draw the flag of our nation and explain the significance of the design.

2. Discuss the role of symbols in the life of a nation.

3. What suggestions would you make for developing national consciousness among our people?

4. Do you consider the national motto, 'Pride and Industry', an apt description of the character of Barbadians?

NATIONAL ANTHEM OF BARBADOS

First Verse

In plenty and in time of need
When this fair land was young
Our brave forefathers sowed the seed
From which our pride is sprung,
A pride that makes no wanton boast
Of what it has withstood
That binds our hearts from coast to coast –
The pride of nationhood

Chorus

We loyal sons and daughters all
Do hereby make it known
These fields and hills beyond recall
Are now our very own.
We write our names on history's page
With expectations great,
Strict guardians of our heritage
Firm craftsmen of our fate.

Second Verse

The Lord has been the people's guide
For past three hundred years
With him still on the people's side
We have no doubts or fears.
Upward and onward we shall go,
Inspired, exulting, free,
And greater will our nation grow
In strength and unity

NATIONAL PLEDGE

I pledge allegiance to my country Barbados and to my flag
To uphold and defend their honour,
And by my living to do credit to
my nation wherever I go.

CHAPTER 10

NATIONAL HONOURS AND DECORATIONS

It is said that a country's greatest asset is its people. In recognition of this fact, some national governments may choose to honour their outstanding citizens by conferring upon them national honours or awards. It is a great privilege for a citizen to be recognized for his or her contribution towards the betterment of the country or community. In Barbados, we have provision for honouring our outstanding citizens through a local system of national awards and honours. Special recognition is given to our citizens who have distinguished themselves in various fields of endeavour, including sports, civic duties and politics. This system was instituted in 1980. Some of the honours include:

1.   The Order of National Hero

2.   Centennial honours

3.   Golden Achievement awards

4.   The Order of Barbados

The Order of National Hero

The Order of National Heroes Act Chapter 399 makes provision for the conferment of the honour of national hero. There are fixed criteria for the conferment of this national honour contained in this legislation. This honour may be conferred by the Governor-General on the advice of the Prime Minister, on citizens who meet prescribed criteria for appointment. This honour may be conferred upon an individual during his lifetime or after he has died.

Criteria for Eligibility

In determining the eligibility of a person for the order of national hero, regard shall be had to the following criteria, whether:

1. the person has given outstanding service to Barbados which has altered the course of the history of Barbados;

2. the person has given service to Barbados which has been exemplified by visionary and pioneering leadership, extraordinary achievement and the attainment of the highest excellence which has redounded to the honour of Barbados or,

3. the person has, through his heroic exploits and sacrifice, contributed to the improvement of the economic and social conditions of Barbados and Barbadians generally.

A person upon whom the Order of National Hero has been conferred is entitled to wear the prescribed insignia of the Order of National Hero and to be referred to as the "Right Excellent".

In Barbados, there are 10 persons upon whom the Order of National Hero has been conferred. Nine of the 10 are deceased. The only living national hero is the Right Excellent Sir Garfield Sobers, who was honoured for his great contribution to the advancement of sports, particularly cricket in Barbados and farther afield.

Below are the short biographies of our 10 national heroes:

National Heroes

1. Bussa

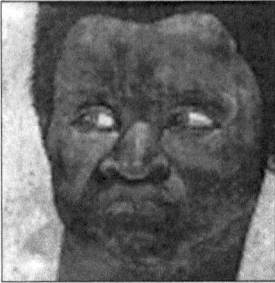

Bussa was born a free man in Africa, but later captured and brought to Barbados to work on the sugar plantations in the late 18th Century. He led Barbados' longest slave revolt in April 1816 against the oppressive white planter class. That rebellion began on Sunday, April 14, 1816 and was the first major uprising in this island since 1692. The revolt was planned, organized and calculated. It was the careful planning of Bussa and other revolutionaries such as Nanny Griggs, a senior domestic on Simmons Estate, which contributed to the effectiveness of this uprising.

Planning for this rebellion had begun after the House of Assembly had discussed and rejected the Imperial Registration Bill in November 1815. By February of 1816, the decision had been made that the revolt would take place in April. On Tuesday, April 16, Bussa led the slaves at Bayley's Plantation into battle. Over 400 of them fought valiantly against the First West India Regiment, but he was killed in battle. Nonetheless, the freedom fighters continued the fight until they were defeated by the armed forces.

Despite the failure of the rebellion, Bussa is to be credited for his leadership and vision in organizing the revolt. In 1985, the Barbados Government recognized his great contribution and unveiled a statue dubbed, 'The Emancipation Statue' in honour of this slave warrior.

2. Sarah Ann Gill (1795-1866)

Sarah Ann Gill, a freed coloured woman was regarded as a heroine of Methodism in Barbados. Gill was born on February 16, 1795. Her contribution to Methodism must be measured in light of the great hostility and censure which pervaded Methodism during the late 18th and early 19th centuries. During this period, Methodists were viewed by the planter class in Barbados as anti-slavery agitators – and, therefore, regarded as enemies of the establishment.

In October 1823, after the Methodist Chapel building was destroyed by a mob of white rioters and the Methodist minister and his wife were forced to flee Barbados, Gill and her sister-in-law were among persons who opened their homes as meeting places for church members.

She held regular worship services in the face of continued opposition and persecution from authorities. Threats were often made against her life and home. She was prosecuted continuously for her defiance of the establishment and was prosecuted in the law courts on two occasions for holding meetings in her home. The holding of such meetings had been declared illegal under the Conventicles Act 1664. This act forbade the assembly of more than five persons for divine worship unless in a licensed meeting place and unless led by a licensed preacher.

On October 19, 1824, the Secret Committee of Public Safety in Barbados declared that they would destroy her home. However, because of condemnation by the Governor, they burnt her effigy instead.

On June 25, 1825, the House of Commons in England declared its utmost indignation for the violation of the law in the colonies, and secured ample protection and religious toleration for all in the colonies. That year, a new Methodist minister was appointed to Barbados, and he built a chapel on land provided by Gill.

Gill died on the 25th February 1866. The headstone of her grave, located at the back of James Street Chapel reads:

Sarah Ann Gill

Died February 25, 1866
Born February 16, 1795

HEROINE OF METHODISM IN BARBADOS
THE DEFENDER OF METHODISM WHEN ITS EXISTENCE
WAS THREATENED IN 1823-1825 WAS PERSECUTED AND
PROSECUTED.

The Gill Memorial Church, built at Fairfield Road, Black Rock, Saint Michael, stands as a monument to the courage, perseverance and commitment of Sarah Ann Gill. It was built in the 1980s to replace the first Gill Memorial Church, built in 1893 at Eagle Hall, St. Michael.

3. Samuel Jackman Prescod (1806-1871)

Described by some as "the Saviour of his country", Samuel Jackman Prescod's mission in life was to improve the conditions of free coloureds and to fight for the emancipation of the slave class.

Prescod was born in 1806 to a free coloured woman and a wealthy land owner and he was named after Samuel Jackman, a rich white planter in Saint Peter. His campaign to enfranchise freed coloureds and blacks began in 1829 when he became editor of the New Times newspaper in March of that year. He later joined the

'Liberal newspaper', which was founded by some poor whites and he spent 20 years educating the masses through this publication.

Prescod was an adept writer and using the skill of his pen, he wrote scathing articles criticizing the planters and accusing them of pursuing policies which suppressed blacks and coloureds.

In 1840, he was charged with criminal libel and jailed for eight days for his criticism of the planter class.

He was responsible for the admission of free coloured people to vote in 1831, and in 1839, he recommended that universal adult suffrage be made law.

On June 6, 1843 Prescod was elected as the first non-white representative to sit in the House of Assembly.

In 1860, he retired from Parliament and was appointed to the office of Judge of the Assistant Court of Appeal. He died on September 26, 1871 at the age of 65 and was buried in the St. Mary's Church yard, Bridgetown.

4. Charles Duncan O'Neal (1879-1936)

Charles Duncan O'Neal was born in 1879 to Joseph and Catherine O'Neal. He attended Harrison College and later Edinburgh University in Scotland, where he studied medicine and gained distinctions including the Blue Ribbon of Surgery.

In 1910, O'Neal returned to Barbados, and raised the social consciousness of the authorities forcing them to pay attention to social ills of the day.

In October, 1924, O'Neal founded the Democratic League. The League's great following was drawn from among the coloured and black classes. O'Neal was greatly concerned about the education of the masses and about politics and he focused much of his energies in these areas. He was the first person to agitate for free education, improved housing and the abolition of the infamous Master and Servant Act in addition to universal suffrage.

In 1932, he won a seat in Parliament and he continued to agitate for improved conditions for workers and for grants for Barbados scholarship winners.

Among O'Neal's great achievements is the creation of a network of grassroots organizations including the Working Men's Association in 1926 and the Democratic League.

His contribution was significant because it was the first time that a man of his stature had put his reputation on the line for the working class and down-trodden.

As testimony to the high regard in which he is held in Barbados, O'Neal's portrait graces the $10 note and the Charles Duncan O'Neal Bridge located on the Wharf Road, Bridgetown, bears his name.

5. Sir Grantley Herbert Adams QC, Kt. Bachelor, CMG (1898-1971)

Born on April 28, 1898, Grantley Herbert Adams often referred to as 'Moses' is hailed as an outstanding Barbadian and spoken of by many with a degree of awe. His vision was to relieve the oppressed masses of their social and economic bondage. Sir Grantley's great vision and political insight led him to become the first Premier of Barbados and the only Prime Minister of the West Indies Federation.

Sir Grantley was a highly respected lawyer and used his great skills of persuasion as a tool to aid him in being elected to the House of Assembly in 1934. He used his debating skills on the floor of the House to challenge the policies of the privileged classes and this gained him the respect and admiration of the masses.

After the 1937 riots, Sir Grantley was sent to England to give evidence before a commission of enquiry into the riots. He used this opportunity to put forward a strong case for reform on behalf of the masses, particularly emphasizing social change and improved conditions for the working class. He also played an integral role in the formation of the Barbados Progressive League, which is now known as the Barbados Labour Party (BLP). In 1940, under his leadership, this party won five of the seats in the House of Assembly. One year later, Sir Grantley formed the Barbados Workers' Union and was its president until 1954.

In 1951, Sir Grantley secured the introduction of universal adult suffrage in the island and later, in 1954, he became the Prime Minister of the West Indies Federation. After the failure of the Federation, Sir Grantley returned home in 1962 and was re-elected to the House of Assembly in 1966 assuming the role of Leader of the Opposition. In 1970, he resigned from public office because of declining health, but remained the president of the BLP. Sir Grantley died at the age of 73 on November 28, 1971.

Among his achievements are:

1.   The introduction of minimum wage legislation

2.   The establishment of housing schemes

3.   The establishment of a wage board and labour department

4.   Universal adult suffrage

5.   The construction of the deep water harbour

6.   The construction of Queen Elizabeth Hospital

7.   The establishment of Erdiston Teachers' College in 1948

8.   The passing of the Workmen's Compensation Act

9.   Improved working conditions for shop assistants.

In recognition of his invaluable contribution to Barbados, National Heroes Day is celebrated on his birthday. In addition, the Grantley Adams' International Airport is named in honour of him as well as the Grantley Adams Memorial School. His portrait is on the country's $100 note.

6. Clement Osbourne Payne (1904-1941)

Clement Osbourne Payne, a Trinidadian by birth, tirelessly advocated the political needs and economic wants of the working class in Barbados. His popular slogan, 'Educate, agitate, but do not violate', was the anthem of the masses.

Payne sought to educate the masses about their lot in life and to urge them to transform themselves into a militant community of workers.

His name is most commonly associated with the riots in 1937 – four days of violence, which was sparked by news of his deportation from the island.

7. Sir Hugh Worrell Springer GCMG, KCMG, GCVO, KA, CBE, OBE (1913-1994)

Sir Hugh Springer was educated at Harrison College. In 1931, he gained a Barbados Scholarship. That scholarship qualified him for entry to Herford College, in Oxford, where he gained a Bachelor of Arts degree in 1936. In 1944, he studied law at the Inner Temple, London, and was called to the Bar in 1938.

Sir Hugh Springer played a pivotal role in the formation of the Barbados Progressive League, a political party of that time, and in 1940 he won a seat in Parliament for St. John.

He was the general-secretary of the Barbados Progressive League, which had created an economic section and later registered as the Barbados Workers' Union.

Sir Hugh Springer helped to lay a solid foundation for the Barbados Workers' Union through his administrative leadership. In 1947, he became the first general-secretary of the union. He served in that capacity until he took up duties as the registrar of the University College of the West Indies at Mona in Jamaica.

Sir Hugh Springer also was a published writer and his work appeared in many regional publications such as The Torch and The Caribbean Quarterly and in some international publications.

In 1984, he was appointed the third native Governor-General of Barbados, a post which he held for six years. He died in 1994.

8. Sir Frank Leslie Walcott Kt. (1916-1999)

Sir Frank Walcott, dubbed the hero of trade unionism in Barbados, served this island's first trade union – the Barbados Workers' Union for 50 years. Through his impressive service, he altered the landscape of trade unionism in Barbados.

Walcott was an outspoken and forceful individual and hailed himself as being 'Frank by name and frank by nature'. Because of his dynamic style, the clerical workers, utility men and government workers joined the union. When Walcott entered the BWU, he only had an elementary school education. However, he used his energies to educate himself and was able to rise steadily through the organization to become its general-secretary.

Walcott distinguished himself both regionally and internationally as a visionary trade unionist. Among the many important positions he held were vice-president of the Executive Board of International

Confederation of Free Trade Unions and president of the Caribbean Conference of Labour for three terms.

From 1958 to 1991, Walcott's labour was concentrated on making the BWU a strong collective bargaining unit and changing the quality of life of the working class in Barbados. In 1966, when Barbados gained independence, Walcott was appointed as this island's first ambassador to the United Nations (UN). He was also responsible for the establishment of the Labour College at Mangrove, St. Phillip, and for organizing a scholarship for members of the BWU and their children. The Sir Frank Walcott Building in Culloden Road, St. Michael bears his name in recognition of his contribution to social security in Barbados. He was a member of the first National Insurance Board and continued to serve on the board for many years.

As a politician, he was elected to the House of Assembly in 1945 and sat in the Upper Chamber in 1966, and again in 1971 to 1976. He was President of the Senate from 1986 to 1991.

9. Errol Walton Barrow P.C., Q.C. (1920-1987)

Hailed as the father of Barbados' Independence, Errol Walton Barrow, popularly known as 'Errol', was one of the premier builders of our Barbadian system of democracy. He was also particularly involved in securing many social changes for Barbados.

Errol Barrow was born in Barbados in the parish of Saint Lucy on the 21st January 1920. During his lifetime, he served as Premier and Prime Minister of this country. He was a founding member of the Democratic Labour Party.

In 1939, he joined the Royal Air Force and served in World War II. After serving in the Royal Air Force, Mr. Barrow studied law and was called to the Bar in 1949. He returned home in 1950 as a practising barrister-at-law and became a member of the Barbados Labour Party (BLP) in 1951. He left this party to help form the Democratic Labour Party in 1955.

In 1961, Mr. Barrow became Premier of Barbados and held that position until 1966, when he took the island into Independence from Britain and became Barbados' first Prime Minister.

Mr. Barrow was twice Prime Minister of Barbados, 1966 to 1976 and then from 1986 to 1987. Mr. Barrow died on June 1, 1987, only one year after regaining the office of Prime Minister following the 1986 general election.

It is said of Mr. Barrow that "he found Barbados a collection of villages, and transformed it into a proud nation", and for that he is truly deserving of the accolade of National Hero. As a further sign of appreciation for his great contribution to Barbados, the birthday of Mr. Errol Barrow is celebrated, annually on January 21, as a national holiday. His portrait also graces this island's $50 note and the Errol Barrow Park in Wildey, Saint Michael, is named after him. On 21st February 2007 a statue in his honour was unveiled in Independence Square, Bridgetown.

His achievements include:
1. The democratisation of our educational system inclusive of free secondary education for all and an improved school meals service.

2. The establishment of the Barbados Community College.

3. The improvement of health care.

4. Designing our modern system of public budgeting and national economic planning.

5. The introduction of a national insurance and social security scheme.

6. Being the architect of the University of the West Indies, Cave Hill campus.

7. Barbados becoming a member of the OAS – Organisation of American States in 1968.

8. Under his leadeship, with two other regional leaders, Vere Bird Sr. of Antigua and Forbes Burnham of Guyana, the Caribbean Free Trade Areas, the forerunner of CARICOM was launched.

9. He led the nation of Barbados into independence on November 30, 1966.

10. Sir Garfield St. Auburn Sobers (1936-)

"When the cricket world discusses the greatest batsmen of all-time, the name Sir Garfield Sobers features prominently in the debate. He is in that short-list which includes Don Bradman, George Headley and Jack Hobbs. When the greatest all-rounders are being discussed, the debate is really about who ranks second behind Garry Sobers."
These words penned by historians, Keith Sandiford and Ronnie Hughes, in their book, 100 Years of Organised Cricket in Barbados, aptly describe the greatness of the man who has been hailed as "The greatest cricketer the world has ever seen".

Garfield Sobers was the fifth of six children born to Sharmant and Thelma Sobers of Walcott's Avenue, Bay Land, Saint Michael on 28 May, 1936.

At an early age, Sir Gary, as he is affectionately known, showed great cricketing promise. From age 13, this cricketing prodigy had caught the attention of cricketing coaches and captains in Barbados were speaking about this young genius. At age 17, he made his international debut for the West Indies in the fifth and final Test against the touring English side, in Jamaica, in March 1954. Sir Gary played international cricket for 20 years and has a very impressive cricketing record. His records, some of which still stand today, include his sixth wicket stand at Lords in 1966 against England. He was also the first batsman to score six sixes in an over in a first-class match, and in

1958, he scored 365 runs not out, which stood for 36 years as the highest individual test score – until it was erased in 1994 by Brian Lara's score of 375.

During his illustrious career, Sir Gary captained the West Indies team; the English county team, Nottinghamshire; as well as the Rest of the World team.

In 1974, Sir Gary retired from international cricket. The following year, he was knighted by Queen Elizabeth II in an open-air ceremony at the Garrison Savannah, in Barbados.

For his contribution to cricket in Barbados and farther afield, a life-size statute of Sir Gary was erected at the Garfield Sobers' Roundabout in St. Michael. In 2007, the statue was removed to the redeveloped Kensington Oval the 'mecca' of cricket in Barbados.

Gold Award of Achievement

The Gold Award of Achievement Act Chapter 401 provides for the conferment of the Gold Award of Achievement on persons who have performed meritorious service to Barbados or to a community within Barbados. This award is conferred annually on National Heroes' Day, on one deserving individual. This honour may be conferred by the Governor-General on the advice of the Prime Minister. It is conferred upon a person, who during the year preceding National Heroes' Day, through his or her diligence, sacrifice, dedication to service, and commitment to excellence, has made an outstanding contribution to community life in Barbados, or to the improvement of the social or economic conditions of the country. A person upon whom the Gold Award of Achievement has been conferred is entitled to have the letters 'GA'. which means, Gold Award of Achievement, placed after his or her name, and to wear, as a decoration, the prescribed insignia for holders of the Gold Award of Achievement.

The Order of Barbados

There are four classes of awards under this order. They are:

1. Knight or Dame of St. Andrew. This award is given for extraordinary and outstanding contributions of service to Barbados, or to humanity at large. A person upon whom this award has been conferred is entitled to have the letters 'KA', which means, Knight of St. Andrew or 'DA', Dame of St. Andrew, placed after his or her name.

2. The Companion of Honour of Barbados (CHB). This award is given for distinguished national achievement and merit.

3. The Crown of Merit. It is made in two grades or categories. The first is the Gold Crown of Merit (GCM) and the other is the Silver Crown of Merit (SCM). This is an award given for highly meritorious service or achievement in the arts, sports, civic duties, literature, science or any other endeavour worthy of national recognition.

4. The Barbados Service Award. This award is made in two grades or categories. These are the Barbados Service Star (BSS) and the Barbados Service Medal (BSM). This award is given for meritorious work in the fire, military, police, civil, prison, and other protective services or any other similar field.

Other awards and decorations may also be conferred. These include the Barbados Star of Gallantry and the Barbados Bravery Medal. There are also some awards and declarations which are made exclusively to members of the Defence Force, the Royal Barbados Police Force, the Barbados Fire Service and the Prison Service for long and faithful service.

CHAPTER 11

OUR CARIBBEAN AND LATIN AMERICAN NEIGHBOURS

CARICOM

Small states have learnt from experience that if they cooperate to form political, economic or other groupings to face their problems, they can be much more effective than if they remain as small single units.

Whatever definition of small we may employ, Barbados is a very small country. Small size renders our nation more vulnerable to external developments than large countries. In an effort to overcome the limitations imposed by small size, Barbados has been an initiator of efforts to attain regional economic integration in the Caribbean.

In 1965 Barbados, Antigua and Guyana came together to establish the Caribbean Free Trade Area (CARIFTA). This constituted a limited, but very important step in economic co-operation among Caribbean countries. We say "limited" because the mere removal of import duties on goods traded among members of CARIFTA, could make little or no impact on the acute problem of chronic unemployment plaguing CARIFTA countries. Subsequent developments in the integration movement have been motivated by the necessity to employ the kind of mechanism which could boost economic development among partners of the integration movement.

This necessity has given birth to the Caribbean Community and Common Market (CARICOM). The member countries of CARICOM are Antigua and Barbuda, Bahamas, Barbados, Belize, Dominica, Grenada, Guyana, Haiti, Jamaica, Montserrat, Saint Kitts and Nevis, Saint Lucia, Saint Vincent and the Grenadines, Suriname and Trinidad and Tobago.

There are five associate members and seven observers. The five associate members are Anguilla, Bermuda, British Virgin Islands, Cayman Islands and Turks and Caicos Islands.

The seven observers are Aruba, Colombia, Dominican Republic, Mexico, Netherlands Antilles, Puerto Rico and Venezuela.

CARICOM aims at:

(1)   The economic integration of the region.

(2)   The establishment and operation of common services.

(3)   Co-ordination of the foreign policy of the independent members.

The Caribbean Community aims at achieving its objectives through:

(1)   The removal of the import duties on goods produced within the community.

(2)   A common external tariff, i.e., the imposition of uniform duties on certain goods coming from outside of the region.

(3)   The co-ordination of national development planning including the joint development of the natural resources of member states.

(4)   The co-ordination of trade between member countries and others which are external to the region.

(5)   The encouragement of inflows of capital, technology and management from the more developed to the less developed countries of the region, as well as the provision of markets in more developed countries.

At present, the Caribbean Secretariat is responsible for the co-operation of tourism services in the area of air transport; as well as other services in education, health, meteorology, and shipping. This regional cooperation assists in preventing duplication of expenditure, as well as allowing member countries to benefit from services which the individual countries could not afford.

CARICOM Single Market and Economy

In 1989, the heads of government of the CARICOM member states decided to deepen their economic ties through the establishment of a single market and economy. The Treaty of Chaguaramas was modified to provide the legal framework for the coming into being of the CARICOM Single Market and Economy (CSME). The CSME provides for the removal of all restrictions to the freedom of movement of capital, labour, goods and services within the single market. It provides for the right of establishment and freedom from discrimination by governments of CSME member states, against nationals of other member states seeking to do business elsewhere in the single market and economy. The implementation of the CSME is scheduled to take place through a series of phases.

The first phase of the deepened integration movement came into effect on 23rd January 2006 when Barbados, Guyana, Jamaica, Trinidad and Tobago, Surinam, and Belize fulfilled the requirements and deposited the legal documents necessary to establish the CARICOM Single Market, (CSM).

At the end of June 2006, six Organisation of Eastern Caribbean States (OECS) – St. Lucia, Dominica, Grenada, Antigua and Barbuda, St. Vincent and the Grenadines, and St. Kitts and Nevis ratified the agreement. At present, there are no restrictions to the freedom of movement of capital, goods and services. The freedom of movement of labour is being implemented on a phased basis. Currently there are no restrictions of movement within the common market area for university graduates, artistes, media workers, musicians and teachers.

Achieving economic cooperation is the main focus of the CSME. To better understand the CSME, two important components – single market and single economy – are defined.

The single market is a market area created by the unification of the national markets of several countries. It is an arrangement which allows CARICOM goods, services, people and capital to move through-out the Caribbean Community without tariffs/barriers and without restrictions so as to achieve a single large economic space, and to provide for one economic and trade policy for all CARICOM states.

The single economy means the creation of an economic space that approximates a single country from the economies of several countries. It is an arrangement in which foreign exchange and interest rate policies, tax regimes, laws and common currency, among other things, are co-ordinated and harmonized. It would also achieve a more level economic performance across CARICOM member states.

It is hoped that the single economy will be established by 2008. A single economy requires the harmonization of social and economic policies as well as legal systems. The complexity of this undertaking suggests that a timeframe of 2008 is somewhat ambitious. The urgency of the integration agenda is being dictated by the rapid pace of globalisation during the last three decades. The emergence of mega-trading blocs such as the European Union, the North American Free Trade Area, the proposed Free Trade Area of the Americas, and the resurgence of the ASEAN bloc further highlight the insignificance of small states, such as those that comprise the CARICOM in the world of international economic relations. A CSME that has a combined population of about six million is still minuscule in light of the magnitude of the mega-trading blocs.

In addition to the forces of globalisation, the phasing out of preferential trade agreements has placed additional pressure on the English-speaking Caribbean states, to solidify their economic co-operation pact in order to provide for growth and development. The CSME lays the framework for maximizing the use of productive resources in the sub-region, and generating greater economies of scale in production, thereby enabling increased penetration of extra-regional export markets and greater capacity to respond to the regional demand for goods and services. A vibrant CSME will challenge our youths to prepare for the new categories of skills that will be required by industry in a modern knowledge economy.

The thinking behind the establishment of the CSME is that the Caribbean states would have more economic and political strength and better prospects, within this type of framework, than they would have if they faced the global economy individually. The central tenor of globalization is the creation of mega-trading blocs such as the WTO, FTAA and EU. Within this global dispensation, the countries of the region will not enjoy any preferential treatment or arrangements as before. Thus "equal competition" becomes the "mainstream". Small developing countries with a small population size and a vulnerable economic and political structure will find it difficult to survive within this arrangement.

The Caribbean Court of Justice

On 4th February 2001, 10 political leaders of the Caribbean region signed the agreement providing for the establishment of the Caribbean Court of Justice (CCJ). This court, with its headquarters in Trinidad, is intended to replace the Privy Council in England as the final court of appeal for the member states of the Caribbean Community which are parties to the agreement establishing the court.

The court was inaugurated on 16 April 2005, with Barbados and Guyana as the only two states which have adopted the CCJ as their final court of appeal. It is hoped that the other Caribbean countries will eventually join the court.

In addition to its appellate jurisdiction, the CCJ has the important role as a court of original jurisdiction to interpret and apply the revised Treaty of Chaguaramas; the treaty which provides the legal framework for the CARICOM Single Market and Economy. It is the CCJ which will settle disputes which might arise among members of the single market and economy, with respect to the matters governed by the treaty.

The agreement establishing the court makes provision for it to be staffed by a President and nine judges. The president is appointed by a majority vote of three quarters of the heads of government of the countries contracting to the agreement, on the recommendation of an independent regional judicial and legal services commission and may only be removed by the affirmative recommendation of the tribunal set up for that purpose. The other judges are appointed and may be removed by the Regional Judicial and Legal Services Commission.

In order to ensure that the court is adequately financed and its independence further protected, the financing of the court is guaranteed by a trust fund of US$100 million, which is invested by the Caribbean Development Bank (CDB).

Caribbean Development Bank

The CDB is a regional institution which was established in January 1970. The bank, which has its headquarters at Wildey in Barbados, has two types of membership: (a) regional, which comprises English, speaking Caribbean territories, Venezuela and Columbia, and (b) non-regional members, which at present are the United Kingdom and Canada.

Article 1 of the agreement establishing the bank, describes its purpose as that of "contributing to the harmonious economic growth and development of the member countries in the Caribbean and promoting economic co-operation and integration among them, having special and urgent regard to the needs of the less developed members of the region".

The bank normally makes loans to its regional members as well as public and private enterprises operating within those countries, to finance projects which contribute to the development of the region or any of the regional members. It has, therefore, provided loans in fields such as agriculture, fisheries, livestock, mining, tourism, low- and middle-income housing.

The bank also provides advisors, consultants and experts on either a long- or short-term basis to assist member countries in identifying suitable projects for financing by the bank, preparing feasibility studies, implementing loan projects as well as training nationals in various economic development activities. Such technical assistance as the

CDB provides is channelled mainly to the lesser developed countries of the region. This group of countries is composed of the Windward and Leeward Islands.

The Caribbean Development Bank is the financial arm of the regional integration movement. Much of its lending takes the form of lending to local institutions, which in turn lend to individuals or groups for specific purposes. It has a soft loan "window" whereby money is lent at low-interest rates and a commercial 'window', where money may be borrowed at market rates.

Caribbean Examination Council

For many years, our school children have written examinations, which were set and marked by examining bodies in Britain. Just as it was thought some years ago that the time had come for us to establish our own university, so it was thought that, at a time when Caribbean people were becoming conscious of themselves as independent persons, school leavers should write examinations planned and set by Caribbean teachers. One advantage of this change would be the development of examinations which would be more relevant to West Indian children. As a result, Caribbean leaders met in Montserrat in 1971 and signed an agreement called the Montserrat Accord, for the setting up of the Caribbean Examination Council (CXC). The council was established in 1972. The first examinations of the Caribbean Examination Council were held in 1979. The members of the CXC are Anguilla, Antigua and Barbuda, Barbados, Belize, British Virgin Islands, The Cayman Islands, Dominica, Grenada, Guyana, Jamaica, Montserrat, St Kitts and Nevis, St Lucia, St Vincent and the Grenadines, Trinidad and Tobago, Turks and Caicos Islands.

The policy-making organ of the organization is the council, which comprises representatives of the regional universities, persons appointed by participating governments and members of the teaching profession of the participating states.

Recommendations on policy and review of the council's work are made by two committees: (a) the Administrative and Finance Committee, which, as its name suggests, is responsible for the general administration of the council's work, and (b) the Schools Examination Committee, which is concerned principally with the preparation of syllabi and the conduct of examination.

The council is administered from its headquarters in Barbados, where the chief officer, the registrar, is based. There is also a Western Zone Office in Jamaica, headed by a pro-registrar, who is responsible for matters relating to the Schools Examination Committee and syllabus formulations.

There are two levels for certification: (a) the Basic Proficiency level and (b) the General Proficiency level. Both of these examinations should normally be taken after five years of secondary education and are graded to show the competence of the school leavers in various subjects. The General Proficiency level is equivalent to the 'Ordinary' level of the General Certificate of Education (GCE) of the English Examination Boards and is recognized by regional universities as well as by many universities overseas.

In 1998, CXC offered the first Caribbean Advanced Proficiency Examination (CAPE) in a range of subjects. The CAPE scheme, which is designed to replace the 'Advanced' level of GCE, is intended to satisfy requirements for entry into regional and extra regional universities as well as other professional courses.

CAPE has been designed to provide an educational experience of intrinsic worth to the student, by developing courses under two main categories: core courses, and academic and vocational courses. These examinations based on common regional curricula, have been an important force for fostering awareness and understanding among students of the importance of the Caribbean in the increasing global arena.

The Organization of American States

The interest of Barbados in regional integration extends beyond the boundaries of the English-speaking Caribbean countries. Barbados regards herself as part of the Latin American region and demonstrates this interest through her participation in activities of the region. Barbados has, for many years, had some contact with her Latin American neighbours; many Barbadians went to Panama to work in the construction of the Panama Canal while others lived in Cuba where they worked on the sugar plantations. The differences in customs and language, however, have over the years prevented the development of closer ties between Barbados and her Latin American neighbours. Today, every effort is being made to overcome these obstacles, and Barbados, as a result of her firm commitment to regional integration, is playing her part in the regional organizations. Prominent among these is the Organization of American States which is a grouping of countries of the Latin American region.

The Organization was founded in 1890 as the International Union of American Republics, and changed its name in 1948 to the Organization of American States. Its chief objective is the promotion of peace and justice: to strengthen collaboration among its members, to defend their sovereignty, territoral integrity and independence, and to advance the economic and social development of the member states. The O.A.S. co-operates with the United Nations in areas of common interest, for example, the Pan-American Health Organization.

The supreme organ of the O.A.S. is the General Assembly, which holds regular sessions once each year. Extraordinary sessions may be held if two-thirds of the members so decide. It is the General Assembly which approves the financial quotas of the member states and sets the general policy of the O.A.S. It is this assembly that facilitates discussion on matters of common interest, be they political, economic, social, cultural or legal.

The General Secretariat is responsible for carrying out the programme of the General Assembly. It is the central and permanent organ of the

O.A.S and is headquartered in Washington D.C. It is headed by a secretary-general who is elected by the General Assembly.

Within the O.A.S., there are other bodies through which various specialized aspects of its work are done. Among these are The Inter-American Juridical Committee, the Inter-American Commission on Human Rights, the Inter-American Court of Human Rights, and the Meeting of Consultation of Ministers of Foreign Affairs.

The Inter-American Juridical Committee is an advisory body and as the name suggests, deals with juridical matters. It comprises 11 jurists, all nationals of member states who are elected by the General Assembly from panels of candidates nominated by member states.

The Inter-American Commission on Human Rights is composed of seven members. It investigates complaints by individuals and institutions of alleged human rights violations. It also prepares studies and reports for distribution to official institutions or civil associations.

The Inter-American Court on Human Rights is an autonomous judicial institution whose purpose is to apply and interpret the American Convention on Human Rights.

The Meeting for Consultation of Ministers of Foreign Affairs is called either to consider problems of an urgent nature and of common interest to the American states, or to serve as an organ of consultation in cases of armed attack or other threats to international peace and security.

Since its admission to the O.A.S. in 1977, Barbados has received various benefits from the organization including fellowships and the provision of experts in different fields.

EXERCISES

1. Write short notes on three of the following:

   (a) CARICOM

(b) Organization of Eastern Caribbean States (O.E.C.S.)

(c) Caribbean Development Bank

(d) Caribbean Examinations Council

(e) Organization of American States (O.A.S.)

2. Discuss the differences between CARICOM and the former West Indian Federation.

3. Why should we buy CARICOM products in preference to those from elsewhere?

4. "A language barrier will always prevent the English-speaking Caribbean from being fully integrated into the Latin American region." Discuss.

5. "The CARICOM Single Market and Economy is of no benefit to the less-developed nations of the Caribbean." Discuss.

6. What are the advantages and disadvantages of free movement within the CARICOM Single Market and Economy (CSME) countries?

7. Make a list of goods which Barbados imports from other CARICOM countries and state the countries from which these items are supplied.

CLASS WORK

1. Prepare a scrapbook containing labels and advertisements for goods imported from other CARICOM countries. Name the country from which each product comes.

2. Draw a wall chart showing the relative value of commercial inputs into your country from CARICOM (indicate the individual countries), other Commonwealth countries, and the rest of the world.

3. Debate this topic: "The English speaking islands of the Caribbean have nothing to gain from association with other Caribbean countries."

CHAPTER 12
OUR RELATIONS WITH THE WORLD

"No man is an island ... every man is a piece of the continent, a part of the main..."

John Donne (1573-1631)

Ministry of Foreign Affairs and Foreign Trade

We live in a world of interdependence. Political independence does not mean that as a nation we are independent of events external to our country. We are affected by developments of an economic and political nature taking place in other parts of the world. In recognition of these facts, Barbados has actively participated in regional and extra-regional organizations.

Before Barbados became independent, its external affairs were conducted by Britain. One of the benefits of Independence is the right to conduct our own external affairs. The most important of these matters are trade and international travel.

Barbados depends upon other countries such as Britain, Canada, the United States of America, Japan and China for many of the things its citizens consume. In recent times, Barbados has strengthened its relations with China, drawing heavily on the Chinese expertise in architecture and building construction to assist it in construction works. Some of this nation's premier buildings, most notably the Garfield Sobers Sports Complex, have been constructed by Chinese workers.

In addition, many Barbadians go overseas to work or study. There are Barbadians in many parts of the world, chiefly in England, the United States of America and Canada. The interests of these Barbadians resident overseas have to be looked after. It is also useful to have representatives abroad to give foreigners information about our country. One benefit of this could be the expansion of our tourist industry and foreign trade.

To look after the needs of the country and to give assistance to nationals living abroad, Barbados like other independent nations, sends representatives to foreign countries; the head of each mission is known as an ambassador. If he is assigned to a Commonwealth country, he is called a High Commissioner. Sometimes the ambassador is away from the foreign country and someone else acts in this place; this person is known as a chargé d'affaires. Other officers who work in the foreign embassies have titles such as minister, counsellor, first secretary and second secretary.

Some officials deal specifically with matters such as granting passports and visas; these officers are known as consuls. The most senior consul in a country is sometimes given the rank of consul-general. Barbados has a consul-general in New York and consuls in some other cities.

It is expensive to maintain embassies; consequently, they are not established in all countries with which we have relations. Another reason why embassies are not established in some countries is that the number of Barbadian nationals or the amount of foreign trade done with those countries does not merit a full-time mission. In such a case, relations with those countries are conducted through the Permanent Mission to the United Nations. Sometimes, the ambassador to one country is accredited to other countries as a non-resident ambassador. For example, the Barbados High Commissioner to London is also Ambassador to France, the Netherlands, and Germany, while the Ambassador to Venezuela is also Ambassador to Brazil.

When our representatives go abroad, they are accorded certain privileges, for example, they do not have to go through normal customs formalities nor can they be arrested and charged before the courts for offences committed in the foreign country unless they agree to submit themselves to the jurisdiction of the courts. This is known as diplomatic immunity. We extend the same courtesies to ambassadors who represent their countries in Barbados. It does not mean that they are free to do as they please, for diplomats are conscious of the fact that they represent their country and they should not bring it into disrepute. In addition, if they misconduct themselves the foreign country can ask that they be recalled.

The embassy of a foreign country is treated as foreign territory. Therefore, if a person seeks refuge in an embassy, the local police cannot enter it to effect his arrest.

The permanent secretary in the Ministry of Foreign Affairs is the administrative head of the Foreign Service. The Ministry of Foreign Affairs keeps in close contact with the representatives abroad and advises them on the Government's policy on various matters, and issue them directives, so that when they speak, they would really be representing the views of the Government.

Ambassadors may be drawn from among career civil servants or may be appointed from among supporters of the party in power. It is customary for politically appointed officers in the Foreign Service to tender their resignations if there is a change of government.

Among the places in which Barbadian Missions are established are London (England), Washington, D.C. (U.S.A.), Ottawa (Canada), and Caracas (Venezuela). There are at present no missions in any of the former communist countries, although Barbados has diplomatic relations with some of these countries.

The United Nations

The United Nations was established on the 24th October 1945 by 51 countries committed to preserving peace through international cooperation and collective security.

When Barbados was admitted to the United Nations on the 9th December 1966, it became the third member of the English-speaking Caribbean to join this big family of over 191 independent nations. The Barbados delegation to the United Nations is led by a senior official whose title is the Permanent Representative to the United Nations.

When states become members of the United Nations, they agree to accept the obligations of the U.N. Charter, an international treaty that sets out basic principles of international relations, the rights and obligations of member states, and the organization's organs and procedures within the United Nations.

Purposes

The United Nations exists mainly to preserve peace in the world; it provides a forum for nations to discuss their problems with a view to settling them peaceably instead of trying to settle them through war. In addition, the United Nations is responsible for facilitating co-operation between member states to solve international economic, social, cultural and humanitarian problems and to promote respect for human rights and fundamental freedoms.

On the admission of Barbados to the United Nations, the then Prime Minister, Mr. Errol Barrow, outlined the stance Barbados would take in international affairs, in the following words:

> *"We have devised the kind of foreign policy which is consistent with our national situation and which is based on the current realities of international politics... we shall not involve ourselves in sterile*

*ideological wranglings because we are exponents
...of the diplomacy of peace and prosperity..., we will
be friend of all and satellites of none. "*

Sometimes persons are heard to say that small nations cannot
influence world politics, but this does not have to be so; for along
with other small nations, Barbados can make its voice heard in the
quest for peace and in trying to get the benefits of this world's goods
more equitably distributed. For many years, Barbados joined in the
condemnation of South Africa's policy of apartheid and supported
the United Nations' attempt to liberate South West Africa (Namibia)
from South African domination. She has also joined the great call
among the poorer countries known as The Third World, for a new
international economic order; this simply means a fairer division of
the world's goods. Through membership of the United Nations,
Barbados is also able to establish political and trading links with
other countries for their mutual advantage.

It must be stressed that the United Nations is not a world government and it does not make laws. This agency operates on a democratic
basis; all the member states, rich and poor, large and small, have a
voice in determining policy and a vote on these policies.

The United Nations has six main organs. Five of them are based
at UN Headquarters in New York; these are the General Assembly, the
Security Council, the Economic and Social Council, the Trusteeship
Council and the Secretariat. The sixth, the International Court of
Justice, is located in The Hague in the Netherlands in Europe.

The General Assembly

The main political organs of the United Nations are the General
Assembly and the Security Council. All members of the United
Nations are members of the General Assembly. The General
Assembly is commonly referred to as a 'Parliament of nations' which
meets to consider the world's most pressing problems. Each member

state has one vote and it is at the meeting of this body that the chief policy statements of various nations are made. Decisions on key international issues which engage the attention of the Assembly are decided by two-thirds majority vote.

Much of the discussion which goes into shaping various United Nations' policies is done in the several standing committees set up by the United Nations. A member country is expected to ensure that its case is heard in the principal committee. The ambassador cannot sit on all the various committees, since many of them meet at the same time; consequently, the work load is shared by his supporting staff.

The Assembly holds its annual regular session from September to December. However, in exceptional circumstances it may become necessary to resume its session or hold a special or emergency session on subjects of particular concern. When the Assembly is not meeting, its work is carried out by its six main committees, other subsidiary bodies and the UN Secretariat.

The Security Council

The body which is chiefly responsible for maintaining peace is the Security Council, which is made up of 15 Council members. Of these, five are permanent members and 10 non-permanent members elected for a two-year period by the General Assembly. The permanent members are China, France, Russia (which holds the seat formerly held by the Soviet Union), the United Kingdom and the United States of America. The Council may convene at anytime whenever peace is threatened. Under the Charter, all Member States are obligated to carry out the council's decisions.

The Security Council has the right to investigate any matter which may cause a disturbance among nations.

The council can take measures to enforce its decisions. In its attempts to preserve peace, it may seek to use persuasion for the cessation of hostilities or it may decide to enforce economic sanctions or order an arms embargo against offending countries. On rare occasions, the council has authorized member states to use "all necessary means", including collective military action, to see that its decisions are carried out.

Decisions of the Security Council require nine affirmative votes for ratification. In order for any resolution to be passed, it must have the approval of all the permanent members since they have the power to veto any resolution. All five members have used the veto at some time or the other. This power is sometimes used to frustrate the wishes of the majority. The following are some occasions on which the veto was used:

- August 2, 1983 – The United States of America vetoed a resolution condemning Israel for its attack on civilians in the occupied Arab territories; the vote was 13 in favour, one against, and one abstention.

- September 12, 1983 – The Soviet Union vetoed the resolution which asked the Security Council to conduct a full investigation into the circumstances surrounding the downing of a Korean airline on September 1, 1983 by Soviet aircraft.

- October 28, 1983 – The United States of America vetoed a resolution calling for the withdrawal of foreign troops in Grenada.

The Security Council sometimes sends a peace-keeping force comprising soldiers from various countries to maintain the peace in troubled areas. Among the areas where the United Nations has had peace-keeping forces are the Middle East and Cyprus.

The Council also makes recommendations to the General Assembly on the appointment of a new Secretary-General and on the admission of new members to the UN.

The Economic and Social Council

The Economic and Social Council is under the authority of the General Assembly. It is responsible for coordinating the economic and social work of the United Nations and the UN family of organizations, formulating policy recommendations and fostering international co-operation for development.

The Council has 54 members, elected by the General Assembly for three-year terms. It meets throughout the year and holds a major session in July, during which a special meeting of ministers discusses major economic, social and humanitarian issues.

The Trusteeship Council

The Trusteeship Council was established to provide international supervision for 11 trust territories administered by seven member states and ensure that adequate steps were taken to prepare the territories for self-government or Independence.

The Trusteeship Council now consists of the five permanent members of the Security Council and it meets whenever the occasion may necessitate the convening of this body.

The International Court of Justice

The International Court of Justice, also known as the World Court, is the main judicial organ of the UN. The court sits at The Hague in the Netherlands. It consists of 15 judges who are elected jointly by the General Assembly and the Security Council. The court hears disputes between countries. Participation by states in any proceeding before this court is voluntary, but if a state agrees to participate, it is obligated to comply with the court's decision. The court also provides advisory opinions to the General Assembly and the Security Council upon request.

On the 7th November 2005, the General Assembly and the Security Council elected five new members to the court, for nine-year terms beginning on 6th February 2006. The newly elected members are Mexico, Morocco, New Zealand, the Russian Federation and the United States of America.

The Secretariat

This body is responsible for the administrative work of the United Nations as directed by the General Assembly, the Security Council and the UN's other organs. It is headed by the Secretary-General.

The Secretariat consists of departments and offices staffed by persons drawn from some 170 countries. The major offices of the Secretariat are located at UN Headquarters in New York, UN offices in Geneva and Vienna; there are also offices in Nairobi and other locations.

UN Agencies

The United Nations does much of its work through its agencies. A short summary of the activities of some of these agencies is given below:

(a)   UNESCO – One of the major agencies is the United Nations Educational Scientific and Cultural Organization. this agency was established in 1946 and gives assistance to member nations in the field of education through the provision of literature, experts, exchanges and grants.

(b)   FAO – The Food and Agricultural Organization, in its effort to ensure that the whole world enjoys a satisfactory level of nutrition, aims at raising and improving the efficiency of the production of food and agricultural products.

(c)   WHO – The World Health Organization was established in 1946 for the purpose of assisting all nations to establish a high level of health. The work of this agency is carried out in Barbados by the Pan American Health Organization (PAHO), an agency of the Organization of American States which works in co-operation with WHO.

(d) UNDP – The United Nations Development Programme was established in 1965 when there was a merger of the United Nations Special Fund and the United Nations Expanded Programme for Technical Assistance.

The UNDP is the most universal of all organizations which grants assistance for development. It co-ordinates the technical co-operation activities of the entire UN family.

The basic objective of the UNDP's work is to help low-income countries to make the best use of both their human and natural resources. Most of its assistance goes to the very poorest of nations. To carry out the objectives, the main services provided by the programme are:

(i) location and development of natural resources, for example, by carrying out surveys on minerals and fuels, land for farming, water for fishing and irrigation;

(ii) the improvement and expansion of educational, vocational and technical training;

(iii) adoption of modern technology;

(iv) improvement of public administration and development planning within the countries which receive assistance.

The programmes of the UNDP are financed partly by the developing countries themselves and partly by voluntary contributions from the vast majority of the member states of the United Nations and its affiliated agencies.

(e) ILO – The International Labour Organization is another United Nations agency of importance to Barbados. Representatives of government, the trade unions and employers' association attend the sessions of the ILO.

Besides providing fellowships for Barbadians, the ILO has been of assistance in providing experts, for example, an expert was made available to advise on some aspects of the National Insurance and Social Security Scheme.

Two other agencies of the United Nations are the World Bank (The International Bank for Reconstruction and Development) and the IMF (International Monetary Fund).

(f)   IBRD – The International Bank for Reconstruction and Development (The World Bank) channels its resources to assist poor countries with their economic development programmes. One of the major problems a small country, such as Barbados, faces in applying for credit from the World Bank is that given the small size of our economy, few projects will qualify for World Bank financing.

(g)   IMF – The International Monetary Fund (IMF) is an important institution for all member countries since it provides support for countries faced with the inability to meet their financial commitments to the rest of the world. The IMF will provide support to deal with temporary or long-term payment difficulties, but it also presents the conditions which are a prerequisite for such support. Countries borrow from the IMF as a last resort since the IMF conditions are very stringent.

In addition, a number of UN offices, programmes and funds, such as United Nations Development Fund for Women (UNIFEM), The United Nations Industrial and Development Organization (UNIDO), The United Nations' specialized industrial agency, the Office of the UN High Commissioner for Refugees (UNHCR), and the UN International Children's Fund (UNICEF) – work to improve the economic and social conditions of people around the world. They report to the General Assembly or the Economic and Social Council.

(h) UNIFEM – was created in 1976 by the UN General Assembly Resolution 31/133. It is the women's fund at the United Nations. It provides financial and technical assistance for programmes to promote women's empowerment and gender equality. UNIFEM focuses its activities on reducing feminized poverty, ending violence against women, reversing the spread of HIV/AIDS among women and girls, and achieving gender equality in democratic governance in times of peace as well as war.

(i) UNIDO – is the mandated organization to promote industrial development and international industrial cooperation. UNIDO works largely in developing countries with governments, business associations and individual companies.

(j) UNICEF provides long-term humanitarian and developmental assistance to children and mothers in developing countries. Its primary focus includes child survival, child education, gender equality, child protection, and HIV/AIDS. UNICEF relies on contributions from governments and private donors. Its programmes emphasize developing community-level services to promote the health and well-being of children.

(k) The UNHCR was established December 14, 1950 to protect and support refugees at the request of a government or the United Nations and assists in their return or resettlement. Its primary purpose is to safeguard the rights and well-being of refugees. It strives to ensure that everyone can exercise the right to seek asylum and find safe refuge in another State.

World Trade Organization (WTO)

Another important international organization of which Barbados is a member is the World Trade Organization (WTO), an international and multilateral organization, which sets out rules and guidelines for the global trade between nations and for the resolution of trade disputes between its member states, all of whom are signatories to its many agreements.

The WTO was established in 1995 to succeed the General Agreement on Tariffs and Trade (GATT). It has 149 members. The primary aim of the WTO is to increase international trade between member states by promoting lower trade barriers and providing a platform for trade negotiations and other trade related affairs. Its main functions are to act as a forum for trade negotiations, to administer trade agreements and to handle trade disputes. The key principles of operation are non-discrimination and ensuring that similar products from different countries are treated in the same fashion on the global market.

The WTO, has four main levels of organization. The first is the Ministerial Conference. This is the decision-making body of the WTO, which meets on a biennial basis. It brings together all the members of the WTO for a meeting on trade issues. The Ministerial Conference is empowered to make decisions on all matters which arise under any of the multilateral trade agreements.

The second level is the General Council Level. The day-to-day operations of the Ministerial Conference are carried out by three groups: the General Council, the Trade Policy Review Body and the Dispute Settlement Body.

At the third level are the Councils for Trade. There are three councils for trade: the Council for Trade in Goods, the Council for Trade-Related Aspects of Intellectual Property, and the Council for Trade in Services.

At the base of this organization are the subsidiary bodies and committees which function under the three councils.

All decisions on trade carried out by the WTO proceed on the basis of five fundamental trading principles. These are as follows:

(a)   A trading system should tend towards more freedom and fewer trade barriers or tariffs.

(b)   A trading system should tend towards greater competition.

(c)   A trading system should be free of discrimination. No one country should privilege a trading partner above another, or discriminate against foreign products or services.

(d)   A trading system should be predictable.

(e)   A trading system should be more accommodating for less developed countries giving them more time to adjust, greater flexibility and more privileges.

The Commonwealth of Nations

Another important international organization of which Barbados is a member is the Commonwealth of Nations. This organization comprises Great Britain and a group of countries all of which were formerly ruled by the British Government, but have since become independent. There are 53 member countries of the Commonwealth. Membership of this body whose membership includes persons of African, Asian and European descent provides Barbados with the opportunity to exchange ideas with countries of different racial and cultural backgrounds spread across millions of square miles. The Commonwealth includes countries such as Canada, Cyprus, Great Britain, India, Jamaica, Kenya, Malawi, Singapore and Zambia.

Various types of parliamentary bodies are found in the countries of the Commonwealth. There are governments with unicameral legislatures. Examples of this form of legislature are found in New Zealand, Guyana, Zambia and Sri Lanka.

Other countries have bicameral legislatures. Barbados is one country with a bicameral legislature; so are Jamaica, the United Kingdom, India, Malaysia and Fiji.

Another difference which exists among the countries of the Commonwealth is that some are monarchies while others are not. Britain, for example, has a hereditary monarchy. Lesotho has a King elected by a College of Chiefs. Others like Barbados, Jamaica, Canada and New Zealand are constitutional monarchies which recognize the Queen as head of state but have a Governor-General as her representative. There is yet another form of government within the Commonwealth, the republican form. The republics have as their head a president. The President may be a ceremonial president whose function is similar to that of a Governor-General or he may be an executive president who is involved in the actual decision-making process of Government. Among the countries which are republics are: Singapore, Guyana, Trinidad and Tobago, Cyprus, Dominica, Kenya and Botswana.

The system of elections in many Commonwealth countries follows the British multi-party system where candidates are selected by two or more parties. In some other countries, Zambia, for example, there is only one legal party in the State.

In some countries, the Upper House is nominated while in others it is elected. In Barbados and Jamaica, members of the Senate are appointed, while in Australia senators are elected with each state having an equal number of senators. India combines the two systems, where the President nominates some of the senators while others are elected.

All member countries of the Commonwealth recognize the Queen as head of the Commonwealth. However, at present, only 15 nations of the Commonwealth recognize the British monarch as their separate head of state.

Members of the Commonwealth keep in touch with one another in various ways. Every two years there is the Commonwealth Heads of Government meeting, which is attended by prime ministers or presidents of the independent members of the Commonwealth. There are also the Finance Ministers' Conference, the Commonwealth Parliamentary Association and the Commonwealth Games. These several activities help to weld the Commonwealth into an influential body of opinion in world matters. For example, the annual Finance Ministers' Meeting takes place just before the yearly meeting of the IMF and World Bank, consequently providing Commonwealth leaders with the opportunity to consult on the major financial issues prior to the meeting of the Fund and World Bank and to arrive at a consensus on important issues.

The main benefit of membership within the The Commonwealth of Nations is the opportunity for close and relatively frequent interaction, on an informal and equal basis, between members who share many ties of language, culture and history.

Another organization which brings the Commonwealth together is the Commonwealth Parliamentary Association. This association was founded in 1911 under the name of the Empire Parliamentary Association. There is an annual conference held in selected Commonwealth capitals. In addition, there are regional meetings and exchange of delegations. The meetings are attended by parliamentarians from both government and opposition. Any country, however, which does not have an elected Parliament, is excluded from the meetings of the association.

The Commonwealth Fund for Technical Co-operation (CFTC) provides technical aid to the developing countries of the Commonwealth. The fund was established to address the dire shortage of high- and middle-level technically trained personnel in many developing countries within the Commonwealth. The CFTC has provided expert assistance to the Caribbean in areas such as agronomy, veterinary science and agriculture generally, as well as in education and health.

The Commonwealth Secretariat with its headquarters in London, England, was created in 1965. It serves all the Commonwealth governments and is responsible for arranging all their meetings. The Secretariat is headed by a Secretary-General who holds office for five years.

EXERCISES

1. Which of the following is the most suitable answer:
   (a) Embassies are established overseas to:
      (i) provide work for party members who do not get elected to Parliament.
      (ii) teach Barbadians how others live.
      (iii) show the world that Barbados is independent.
      (iv) to provide representation for our citizens overseas.

   (b) The United Nations serves as a forum where
      (i) nations seek to solve world problems in a peaceful manner.
      (ii) the big nations teach small nations how to govern themselves.
      (iii) independent countries pass laws to govern the world.
      (iv) small nations are freed from colonialism.

2. What benefits do you think Barbados receives from having established missions overseas?

3. "Barbados is too small to influence world opinion." Discuss.

4. "The United Nations is nothing more than a talk shop." Discuss.

5. Do you think there are benefits to be gained by being a member of the United Nations? Discuss.

6. Who is Barbados' Ambassador to the United Nations? How is his role at the UN beneficial to Barbados? Discuss.

7. Do you think there are benefits to be gained by Barbados by being a member of the Commonwealth of Nations? Discuss.

8. Explain the term 'foreign policy' and list some of the influences which affect the foreign policy of Barbados.

9. Write short notes on the following:
   (i) The UN General Assembly
   (ii) The World Trade Organization
   (iii) The Commonwealth of Nations
   (iv) The Commonwealth Parliamentary Association
   (v) The free trade area
   (vi) Common market
   (vii) Single market

10. What is the International Monetary Fund? Give an account of its main purposes and how they are carried out.

11. What are the functions of the World Intellectual Property Organization and International Fund for Agricultural Development?

12. What is the difference between the World Bank and the International Monetary Fund? Which do you think is more important to your country?

THINGS TO DO

13. Discussion: "The IMF conditions for giving aid are too stringent for small countries."

14. Discussion: "All disputes between countries should be taken to the International Court of Justice as of right; the power of the

court to hear matters of international importance should not be dependent on the willingness of countries to participate in this exercise."

15. Organize a class debate on the moot:

"Overseas missions are a financial burden on the Government of Barbados and should be abolished."

CONCLUSION

In this book, we have examined some of the characteristics of a good citizen. It should be the aim of all of us to be good citizens wherever we live, but there should be special pride in and love for our native land – Barbados.

In this country, every citizen is guaranteed certain rights and privileges, but it is always good to remember that freedom does not imply licence to do always as we like. At times, it is necessary to restrict some individual freedom in the interest of the common good. What do you think would happen if we were all free to drive our vehicles as fast as we wish or to drive them on any side of the street that pleases us? There would be obvious chaos.

The Government imposes certain restrictions on our use of private property. For example, we are required to seek permission from the Town and Country Planning Department before we erect a house on our own land. The Government can acquire our property compulsorily if it is needed for some purpose in the interest of the nation; but the constitution provides for us to be compensated if this is done. At Customs, government officials are authorized to search our luggage, and if the police have good cause, the law permits them to search our homes. At times, we are even forbidden from doing as we please with our own bodies; for example, the taking of certain drugs is illegal.

In spite of these restrictions which are necessary for the common good, we live under a system which affords great freedom of speech and action. We should not take this for granted, but exercise great vigilance, for the price of liberty is eternal vigilance. By being vigilant we can ensure that too much power is never concentrated in the hands of too few who claim to exercise it on behalf of us all.

We should take an interest in how our country is governed at an early age. Young people must take their responsibilities very seriously and know their rights and responsibilities and ensure that their freedom is not gradually eroded. One way of doing this is by keeping abreast of events and working through organizations to influence public policy.

One of the most reliable resources of a country is its young people. It is they on whom the whole future depends. The young people, therefore, should grasp every opportunity for self-improvement, for in so doing the continued development of our nation will be assured.

With adult suffrage, governments have become more sensitive to the needs of the masses and this has resulted in the rapid growth of opportunities for all sections of the society. To whom much is given, much is expected. A society, therefore, which puts more and more of its resources into developing the talents of the young, should expect the youth to respond positively to the opportunities afforded.

It is hoped that by the time you have completed this book, you would have understood something of how our country functions, why we should be proud of our heritage and why we should have a deeper sense of responsibility for the proper functioning of the Government. All citizens should by now be aware of the need to develop attitudes which make for good citizenship and to contribute to the well-being of the society. Mention has been made of our transition from slave society to independent nation. We cannot afford to continue to blame our present deficiencies on slavery, much as that institution has influenced our development. We must attempt to understand our institutions and how they developed, and continue to improve them so that they can meet our needs in the task of nation building.

Each citizen is his brother's keeper. The task of national development requires mutual support.

Let us therefore go forward together, living up to our national motto, "Pride and Industry".

ESSAY TOPICS

1. Write a letter to your Member of Parliament pointing out some need in your district.

2. "Electors should have the right to recall legislators with whose performance they are dissatisfied." Discuss.

3. What part ought the press to play in nurturing a democracy?

4. "The good citizen is the life blood of democracy." Do you agree?

5. Do you think that the Barbados Constitution should be amended? If so, why do you consider these amendments necessary?

6. What in your opinion constitutes the ideal parliamentary representative? Substantiate your stand.

7. Write a letter to a penpal telling him/her how a law is passed in Barbados.

8. The role of trade unions in our society.

9. The value of our national symbols.

10. Write a letter to a friend explaining the various ways in which one can become a citizen of Barbados.

11. Do you consider the jury system a satisfactory mode of trial?

12. What do you understand by the term "Democracy"? Do you consider this a desirable form of Government?

13. "Persons should be elected to Parliament because of their personal qualities and not because of their party affiliations". Discuss.

14. "Political parties should be outlawed since they serve to create divisions in the society". Discuss.

15. "Parliamentary elections should be held at fixed intervals of five years and at no time before the appointed date should the Prime Minister have the power to call General Elections." Discuss.

16. Discuss the advantages and disadvantages of a coalition government.

17. What are the advantages and disadvantages of a written constitution?

18. Show how the appointment of the ombudsman can serve to safeguard our democratic rights.

19. Describe the characteristics of a good citizen.

20. Explain the rights and responsibilities of a citizen.

21. Suggest some ways in which a citizen can serve his community.

22. Show clearly what an individual can learn from his different relationships within the following:
    (a) home
    (b) peer group
    (c) community

23. "Once a citizen, always a citizen." Discuss.

QUIZ

1. Who was the first Governor-General of Barbados?

2. Who was the first native Governor-General of Barbados?

3. Who is the Speaker of the House of Assembly?

4. Who is the President of the Senate?

5. How many members comprise the Senate?

6. Name the members of the Cabinet who are in the Senate.

7. Who is the Minister responsible for Sport?

8. What is a bicameral legislature?

9. When was adult suffrage introduced in Barbados?

10. Who is Chief Justice of Barbados?

11. Who was the first Prime Minister of Barbados?

12. Name six countries which are members of the Commonwealth.

13. When did Barbados become independent?

14. Name three West Indian islands that are members of the United Nations.

15. Who is Secretary-General of the United Nations?

16. Who is the president of the Caribbean Development Bank?

17. Where is the headquarters of the
    (a) Caribbean Tourism Research Centre?
    (b) CARICOM?

18. What is the meaning of the A.C. P. Countries?

19. What do the following mean
    (a) I.L.O.
    (b) U.N.D.P.
    (c) U.N.I.C.E.F.
    (d) F.T.A.A.
    (e) W.H.O.

20. (a) Name three things that member countries of the Commonwealth have in common.
    (b) Name five statutory corporations.

21. What is the significance of the broken trident on our nation's flag?

22. The press is sometimes called the 'Fourth Estate'. What are the other three 'estates'?

23. Who is the Secretary-General of the Caribbean Secretariat?

24. Why is our type of government known as the 'Westminster Model'?

25. What is the meaning of
    (a) W.H.O.?
    (b) P.A.H.O.?
    (c) U.N.E.S.C.O.?
    (d) W.T.O.?
    (e) F.T.A.A.?

26. Name three posts in the civil service that are specially provided for in the constitution.

27. Who designed the Barbados Flag?

28. Who wrote the words to the National Anthem?

29. Who composed the music to the National Anthem?

30. Who designed the Coat of Arms?

31. How are permanent secretaries appointed?

32. What is the name of the trade union that represents the majority of civil servants?

33. Which trade union in Barbados has the largest membership?

34. How many constituencies are there in Barbados?

35. How is the Prime Minister chosen?

36. What is proportional representation?

37. How many members sit on a jury?

38. When was adult suffrage introduced into Barbados?

39. Name two Spanish-speaking countries which are members of CTRC.

40. Who is the Secretary-General of the OAS?

41. Which is the highest post in the OAS ever held by a citizen of a country of the English-speaking Caribbean? Who was that person?

42. Name one non-regional member of the Caribbean Development Bank.

43. In what year was the first meeting of the Parliament of the short-lived Federation of the West Indies?

44. Who were the first representatives from Barbados to the Federal Parliament?

BIBLIOGRAPHY

1. **Cohen N.E.,** *The Citizen Volunteer* – Harper & Bros Publishers, N.Y. 1960

2. **Douglas P & McMahon,** *How to be An Active Citizen* – University of Florida Press 1960

3, **Emmanuel Patrick A.M.,** *Elections and Party Systems in Commonwealth Caribbean* – Caribbean Development Research Services (Barbados) 1992.

4. **Hoyos F. A.,** *Barbados, A History from the Amerindians to Independence* – McMillan Education Ltd. 1978

5. **Jacobsen GA & Lipman M.H.,** *Political Science* – Barnes & Noble, Inc. N.Y. 1951

6. **McDonald Neil,** *The Study of Political Parties* – Random House N.Y. 1951

7. **Mark Francis,** *History of Barbados Workers Union* – Pub. Barbados Workers Union

8. **Ruddock,** *Civics for Young Jamaicans* – Collins 1967

9. **Silvert Kalman H.** *The Reason for Democracy* – The Viking Press New York, 1977

ABOUT THE AUTHOR

W. LeRoy Inniss is a retired judge of the High Court of Barbados. He holds a B.A. degree in Spanish, a Diploma in Education from the University of the West Indies, and an LL.B. degree from the University of London.

He has taught in the Turks & Caicos Islands where he was head-master of the Grand Turk Secondary School. He was also head of the Department of Law at the Barbados Community College.

Mr. Justice Inniss is a Queen's Counsel and is a past president of the Barbados Bar Association. He is a former member of the Senate of Barbados. His publications include *Civics for the Eastern Caribbean* and *The Constitution and You – Barbados.*

www.ingramcontent.com/pod-product-compliance
Lightning Source LLC
Chambersburg PA
CBHW060849280326
41934CB00007B/972